CISTERCIAN FATHERS: NUMBER FORTY-THREE

John of Ford

Sermons on the Final Verses of the Song of Songs

Volume Three

(Sermons 29–46)

Translated by
Wendy Mary Beckett

α

Cistercian Publications
cistercianpublications.org

LITURGICAL PRESS
Collegeville, Minnesota
litpress.org

A Cistercian Publications title published by Liturgical Press

Cistercian Publications
Editorial Offices
161 Grosvenor Street
Athens, Ohio 45701
cistercianpublications.org

The editors wish to express their appreciation to Mr. John Nixon for his help in preparing the manuscript for publication.

This translation is based on the critical Latin edition of the sermons prepared by Edmund Mikkers and Hilary Costello and published in the series CORPUS CHRSTIANORUM, *Continuatio Mediaevalis* XVII & XVIII.

Latin title:
Ioannis de Forda, Super extremam partem cantici canticorum sermons cxx.

© 1982 by Cistercian Publications. © 2008 by Order of Saint Benedict, Collegeville, Minnesota. All rights reserved. No part of this book may be used or reproduced in any manner whatsoever, except brief quotations in reviews, without written permission of Liturgical Press, Saint John's Abbey, PO Box 7500, Collegeville, MN 56321-7500. Printed in the United States of America.

ISBN 978-0-87907-446-3

Library of Congress Cataloging-in-Publication Data (Revised)

John, Abbot of Ford.
  Sermons on the final verses of the Song of Songs.

  (Cistercian Fathers series ; no. 29, 39, 43)
  Translation of Ioannis de Forda Super extremam partem Cantici canticorum sermones CXX.
  On Spine: on the Song of Songs.
  Includes bibliographical references.
  CONTENTS: 1. Sermons 1-14—2. Sermons 15-28
  1. Bible.   O.T. Song of Solomon–Sermons

  1. Bible.   O.T. Song of Solomon–Sermons.
  2. Catholic Church–Sermons.   3. Sermons, English–Translations from Latin.   4. Sermons, Latin–Translations into English.   I. Title.
  II. Title: On the Song of Songs.

BS1485.J6413   223'.907   77-3697
ISBN 978-0-87907-643-6 (v. 1)   AACR1

Book design by Gale Akins

TABLE OF CONTENTS

SERMONS

Sermon Twenty-Nine	1
Sermon Thirty	12
Sermon Thirty-One	25
Sermon Thirty-Two	38
Sermon Thirty-Three	50
Sermon Thirty-Four	62
Sermon Thirty-Five	72
Sermon Thirty-Six	84
Sermon Thirty-Seven	94
Sermon Thirty-Eight	104
Sermon Thirty-Nine	115
Sermon Forty	124
Sermon Forty-One	134
Sermon Forty-Two	147
Sermon Forty-Three	156
Sermon Forty-Four	167
Sermon Forty-Five	179
Sermon Forty-Six	191

SERMON TWENTY-NINE

That the belly of the spouse is rightly to be understood as the love which draws him to the bride, just as the 'belly' of the bride is the love that draws her to the spouse. But she calls it 'a block of ivory, for this is a chaste love, and as pure as it is lovely. And indeed it is 'studded with sapphires', to indicate the many different joys she finds in him.

'HIS BELLY A BLOCK OF IVORY, studded with sapphires.'*   *Sg 5:14*
In the previous sermon, we were given the grace to discuss, while you charitably bore with us, 'the belly of the spouse', thinking of the attitude of tenderness which makes him yearn like a father or mother towards us, his children. And for this twofold love I confess I am bound by a double debt, one of love and honor. It involves me in love, because, among all the emotions of the human heart, it is love alone that surges up to pay a debt like this, although it can never do more than make some beginning of repayment. Yet honor, too, for a law has been set before me, written by the finger of God himself, telling me to 'honor my father and my mother'.*   *Cf. Ex 20:12*
do this, I have a firm promise made me, that all will go well for me and I shall have a long life.* So I acknowledge a double debt of love   *Cf. Sir 3:6*
and honor because I have been adopted in a

double way, and he who laid the obligation upon me, will see to it that I make repayment. Indeed, seeing that he has made himself both father and mother to me, he will also make me into his true son, through the Spirit of adoption.* *Cf. Deut 5:16*

Now, if there is such tenderness of love in his heart, flowing out to his children, what must we think of the overflowing tenderness he must feel for his bride?

2. I cannot believe that the thought of that heart of his, played no part in the bride's mind when she here speaks in praise of his 'belly'. We know, in fact, that in the whole range of human relationships, there is none more passionate than that intimacy with which spouse and bride give themselves to each other. It takes precedence even of the love that unites children to their parents or parents to their children. It takes the precedence, let me repeat, and far outdistances it, seeming to gather strength while parental love grows weak. For when a man has taken a wife to his bosom, whatever love he had for parents or other intimates, becomes drowsy and ineffectual. So 'the belly of the Spouse' can rightly be taken as meaning that passionate tenderness which he feels for his bride, as phrase upon phrase in this Song of Songs makes incontrovertibly clear.

The spouse himself is quite unable to conceal this tenderness from the bride. Since he is a spouse, he does not only know her as a spouse, but he speaks to her as a spouse, and acts towards her in all respects as befits a spouse. If, for the time being, the full force of his charm must remain hidden from the little ones, because they have not the capacity to receive it, surely this is not so for the bride? He comes forth from his Father, and whatever he has heard from his Father, he whispers intimately to his beloved.* What he has learnt in the bosom of the Father, overflows into the bosom of his beloved.* There is no point, here, in concealment. The veil has been taken away, and the bride approaches her spouse in utter confidence. She is wholly free to gaze with unveiled countenance upon the glory of the Father's only Son, and all her desire to be transformed into his likeness.* For his part, the spouse refuses nothing she asks, and he leaves his beloved free to act towards him as lovingly as she wishes.

Cf. Jn 15:15

Cf. Jn 13:25

Cf. 2 Cor 3:18

But it is more than just a matter of granting her wishes: he surrenders himself to his bride to be spoken to and to be experienced in his fragrance, to be kissed and to be embraced, and finally, to be held to her heart. For it is after experiencing all the joys which, as we said above, she had prayed for, that the bride cries out to the maidens, 'I hold him, and I will not let him go.'* And the spouse, on the other hand, surely what he says will be, 'My heart has become like wax, melting within my belly'?* Because as far as he is concerned, everything gives way to the wishes of his bride, and it is his good pleasure that she should take her pleasure of him. Why should his heart not have melted, since he himself tells us that the bride has wounded it? 'You have wounded my heart,' he says, 'my sister, my bride, you have wounded my heart.'*

Sg 3:4

Ps 22:14

Sg 4:9

Moreover, the bride has a witness within her own self, for her belly trembles at the touch of the spouse, and from this instance it is clear to her how the belly of the spouse is likewise affected by her touch, since it is one and the same spirit of love that affects their mutual relationship. How blessed the belly which so great a lover was pleased to touch with his hand and lovingly excite with his touch! And no less powerful the right hand which was able in its turn to touch the belly of its beloved and deeply affect his heart.

When the bride is touched like this, and immediately her whole being trembles with joy, have we not a fulfillment of those words of Jesus, when he promised to give his Spirit? He spoke of rivers of living water that would flow from the belly of the one he loved.* As regards the spouse, there is now no reason why this gift should be held back, as it was on that long ago day. It was a great feast day, and he rose to his feet to cry out the same words and to invite all who thirsted to come to the waters. The evangelist tells us, therefore, that the reason why the Spirit had not yet been given, was 'that Jesus had not yet been glorified.'* But the position of the spouse and his bride is very different. For now Jesus has been glorified, and he has shown himself in his bride's heart. This is why he has given her his Spirit in such abundance and why he has made the waters of his delight spring forth, as he promised, from her belly. That these rivers flow out from the belly of Jesus into the belly of his beloved can only

Sermon Twenty-Nine

be doubted by someone who is ungrateful for this favor, or has never experienced it.

3. Even we who have deserved at least to thirst after this living water, even if we are not among the thirsty who hasten at Jesus' invitation but rather search listlessly for it, nonetheless we return only to this belly, the fount of the same streams and the vein of living waters. Listen to the promise his Father made to the spouse, that he would bless his belly. 'The Lord swore an oath, and he will not take it back: I shall set upon your throne the fruit of your belly.'* Probably you will rejoin that this promise was made to David with reference to his son, the Lord Jesus. I do not deny it, the mystery of the sacred incarnation was promised in these words. Nevertheless, while fully granting that the oath has this meaning, the true David was the man whom the Father found 'after his own heart',* and anointed with his holy oil more than all his fellows.* So there is little doubt that the promise was made to Christ, also. So the Father has solemnly sworn to his only Son a completely new and, as far as we can understand it, completely indescribable oath, namely, that he would set upon his throne the fruit of his belly.

Ps 132:12

Cf. Acts 13:22
Cf. Pss 89:21, 45:7

Rejoice, lift up your heart, daughter of Zion, bride of my Lord, because this promise of honor and the honor of this promise concern you as well!* The fruit of the belly of your spouse is in fact the fruit of your belly. It is obvious that you can only become fruitful through his fruitfulness, but his fruit, coming into you and coming out from you, is

Lam 4:21

the same thing, that is, the fruit of you both. And what is this if not love, joy, peace, and the fruit of holiness which rises from them, that is, the holy generation of their sons and grandsons?* Blessed, O bride, is the fruit of your belly,* yes, and the fruit also of your spouse's belly, because together with this fruit of yours you will reign with your spouse in his kingdom and sit down with him on the throne of his glory. The Lord swore an oath to his Christ, and he will not go back on it.* Rejoice and take courage, for it will all come to pass.

Listen to your spouse promising the same thing in another place: 'If anyone conquers,' he says, 'I shall grant him to sit with me upon my throne, as I have conquered and sit upon my Father's throne.'* You are probably very eager to find out, and burning to know, what exactly is meant by this surpassing glory, to sit down with the only Son of God on his exceedingly lofty and sublime throne. But it is as much as I can do to make even the smallest effort at handling something so bewilderingly great. It is by begging, praying, loving and longing that you and I will come more easily and happily to some understanding of it. These are mysteries of the sacred marriage chamber, and it is not fit that they should be dwelt upon in any sermon of mine. None but the only Son of God can speak worthily of matters such as these.

4. Well then, let us rather turn our attention to why the bride chose to describe the belly of her spouse as 'a block of ivory'. Why not a fleshly adjective instead of one hard as

Cf. Gal 5:22
Cf. Lk 1:42

Cf. Ps 110:4

Rev 3:21

Sermon Twenty-Nine

bone, especially as her intention was to signify charity, in all its gentleness and tender love? In this way, the Lord promised to give us a heart of flesh when he took away from us our heart of stone, meaning he would give us charity, tender and quick to know itself pierced by the wounds of loving grief and holy affection.* *Cf. Ex 11:29*

Surely she called the belly 'a block of ivory' to show that the charity of the spouse is loving indeed, but it is chaste? For ivory is by nature white, or over the years acquires a rosy glow, and in either case is a fitting symbol of chastity, white from its innate lustre and glowing from its outstanding sense of modesty. Moreover, the class of animal, whose teeth are ivory, is said to be uniquely chaste, and after becoming once pregnant, to hold aloof from any other, as if the one and only reason for copulation was simply this, the hope of having offspring. So the bride speaks of ivory to show us very beautifully the incorruptible chastity of her spouse. From his very conception, chastity grew together with him in his mother's womb, and he had the inherited and imperishable glory of receiving a virginal purity both within the virgin and from her.

The bride is taking a wise precaution, then, in case someone bends to this love-song an ear wanting in modesty and 'unclean'. So she is careful to call the belly of her spouse 'a block of ivory', and 'with the sword of the Spirit, which is the word of God,'* she joins Simon Peter in cutting off any 'unclean' *Eph 6:17* ear.* Those who savor the joys of Christ's love only in a manner that is still childish and sensual give sufficient proof to her that they are fleshly, that they are Jewish and uncircumcised, that their palate is too immature for them to be followers of Christ. On the contrary, they persecute him. It is a very good thing for a man like this to be deprived of this Jewish and uncircumcised ear! Then the Lord Jesus engrafts a new ear into him, and he passes from the spirit of slavery into the freedom of being an adopted child of God.* And so, after Jesus had healed the man whose ear Peter had cut off, the evangelist adds significantly, 'And the servant's name was Malchus.'* Malchus, in fact, means 'about to be a king', which clearly implies the freedom of God's sons.

Now that Malchus is healed, let him learn to see nothing in the belly of the spouse but an ivory whiteness and to appreciate his love as being as pure as it is sweet. The love of Christ is a strong and very chaste pleasure. Into it there enters nothing defiled,* nothing enervating, nothing weak, nothing sensual. When that true bride of Christ, St Agnes, sang the praises of her spouse in her wedding song, how fitting that she too should say of him: 'When I have loved him, I am chaste; when I have touched him, I am pure; when I have taken him to myself, I am a virgin.'* Therefore the bride took care to praise the love of her beloved as being as pure as it is tender, as strong as it is sweet, as red-hot yet still ice-cold, all-delight, yet all-holy. Such holiness in the midst of sweetness and such

Cf. Lk 22:50

Cf. Rom 8:15

Jn 18:11

Cf. Wis 7:25

*Responsory from the first nocturn of Vigils for the Feast of St Agnes (Jan. 21) in the Cistercian office.

sweetness in the midst of holiness was wonderful for her to contemplate. By saying 'belly,' she means a real, human love, and by adding 'a block of ivory', she underlines that it must be thought of as having all the qualities of bone.

5. Furthermore, when she goes on to speak of the belly as 'studded with sapphires,' she is not only describing charity as like a bone, but almost as like a stone. And love is indeed a gemstone, taking all emotions to itself and making them insensible of any other attraction whatsoever. O, how precious are stones like this! Anyone who finds them immediately sheds his sensual way of responding to things and takes on instead what one might call the loveliness of a serene heaven. A fruitful field to find these stones, if we are to believe the bride, is none other than the ivory belly of the spouse, that is, the holy and unfeigned charity of Christ. And we know that they are indeed at hand there for the bride, because the belly of the spouse lies open to her chaste hands, in the freedom of the marriage bond. He offers his very belly, not only for her to come close to it, but for her to caress.

Moreover, the sapphire stone has this quality, that just as it has the most delightful color of serenity, so also it has the property of being very effective against the disease of wickedness. And is there anything more wicked than envy, which pines away when all goes well and takes great delight in seeing them go amiss? Among the properties of charity, the apostle gives first place to its power of rooting out the spitefulness of envy, for he says, 'Charity is not envious.'* [1 Cor 13:4]

6. The bride speaks of a 'studding' with sapphires, suggesting that there are very many of them and all different. I think she wanted to symbolize the grace of the different consolations with which she is often most joyfully visited by her spouse, and the joy takes different forms. Who could number them or say what they were like, except perhaps the blessed one who experiences them? In fact, it was her wish to tell us nothing about it, except only this, that in the belly of her spouse these stones are studded. But what form this studding takes, she judges should not be revealed to our ears either from a sense of modesty or because of the limits of our understanding. If anyone thinks it a valuable thing to learn, let him give himself to it and experience it! Let him yearn and pray unceasingly, and exercise himself in this matter of charity. Let him give no sleep to his eyes, no rest to his eyelids.* [Cf. Ps 132:4] Let him give no rest by night or day to the God of peace and love, until the love of Christ comes forth to him from out his bridal chamber, and bursts into flame before him, like a burning lamp. Then the love of Christ will be with him very often, 'coming out to meet him like an honored mother.'* [Sir 15:2] Love will multiply its consolations and come in an infinite variety of ways. When that day comes, blessed experience will make what is heard meaningful, and to every soul who is so disposed it will be clear what is meant by this studding of the spouse's belly with gems as blue as the

sky of heaven: There will be no need then for anyone to ask the spouse any questions.* *Cf. Jn 16:30*

May it be granted us to know this experience and to understand what we hear, through the grace of the spouse of the Church, Our Lord Jesus Christ, who with God the Father and the Holy Spirit lives and reigns,
God, for ever and ever.
Amen.

SERMON THIRTY

The beginning of the thirtieth sermon. In praise of the patience of the Lord Jesus, which is signified by Moses when he speaks of the legs or the bone of the lamb, which is not to be broken. How greatly the church of the nations ought to be attached to him, because when the first bride was sent away in disgrace, she was called to the dignity of marriage with the Lord Jesus, through no merits of her own.

Sg 5:15

'HIS LEGS ARE ALABASTER columns, set in sockets of pure gold.'*
In accordance with the order which the bride is following, it is quite right and fitting that she should pass from praising her spouse's belly to praising his legs, but we must leave it to her judgment her praise is perfectly in keeping with the note of modesty throughout. We must admit, that had the bride paid heed to human modesty or prudence, she would at this stage have put her finger to her lip and, by her chaste reserve, offered greater tribute in silence than she does by public proclamation. If we may take the liberty of asking you about this, O bride of my Lord, what is your intention when you speak these words of praise? Why do you not spare your words, or even spare the ears of the maidens, or, at the very least, spare the honor

of him whom 'your soul loves'?* Where, O fairest of women, is that unmistakable sign upon your cheeks, in which your spouse takes such delight, the noble and lovely radiance of your modesty?

Sg 1:7

In turn, it seems to me that I hear the Spirit of her spouse making answer for his bride and within her. Let the bride then take courage in the Holy Spirit, let her take courage and give an answer. 'If I seem foolish in your eyes, O maidens, understand that the charity of Christ drives me forward.* Where there is the Spirit of my beloved, there is freedom.* It was he who put the words of this holy song upon my lips, words that can be entrusted only to the chaste ears of those who also know Jesus by experience. These are sacred and burning phrases, which the fire of divine charity has refined from all impurity, which only the zeal of lovers has the real right to hear and savor. They are wholly removed, wholly and utterly, from flesh and blood, wholly removed from all that is uncircumcised and unclean. Let dogs stand at the gates, let beasts keep far off, lest any of them should come too close, and touch this burning of charity, in bestial manner, that is, with his sensual understanding and feelings, and according to the law be stoned.* So if any foolish woman has taken scandal at my eulogy, she is like Michol, who of old took scandal at David's dancing naked before the ark.* She then bears witness to her own self, that she has not yet learned to love, if up to now a beloved so beautiful or anything about him, has caused her embarrassment. For

Cf. 2 Cor 5:14

Cf. 2 Cor 3:17

Cf. Heb 12:20

Cf. 2 Sam 6:16

indeed, those who love the name of Jesus know only peace, there is no scandal for them in these words, but only joy and an enkindling of holy love.'

2. Come then, under the guidance of the Holy Spirit, let us go nearer to the marriage chamber of the spouse and the bride. Perhaps, from there, the meaning of these words may become audible to us.

Indeed, with regard to 'the legs of the spouse', I cannot recall any place in sacred scripture where I have heard anything that could be set under this heading. The only exception is when they come to Jesus on the cross to break his legs.* When they saw he was already dead, 'they did not break his legs,'* because the law about the ceremonial observance of the Passover bound them strictly that not a bone of the lamb was to be broken.* But the gospel goes on to say that, instead of breaking his bones, an opening was made in Jesus' side, and immediately blood and water flowed out.* So the bride has every right to take into her song of praise these legs of her spouse, which even the wickedness of his crucifiers feared to harm and which the goodness of Moses the lawgiver preserved from harm.

But was it that Moses prevented this act by his law, or was it not rather, that he declared it to men by his prophecy? My opinion is this, that even then Moses saw beforehand the glory of the Father's only Son. Under the influence of the same Spirit through whom he told how heaven and earth and all things visible and invisible were created, he reverently wrapped round the invincible patience of the Son the holy veil of these words.* 'Not a bone of his is to be broken,' he said. It was as if he lifted up his eyes to that 'stiffnecked' people,* and saw their hands all stained with the sinless blood of the true Lamb. As if he saw that their hunger would not yet be satisfied by devouring the whole Lamb, he cried out a rebuke against them, lashing them with fierce words as was his custom: Ah, but you are a sinful people, a race of evildoers, the offspring of iniquity!* Upon you, by God's irrevocable decree, will come not only all the innocent blood that has been shed on earth,* but also the blood of the Lamb of God, the blood of the Father's only Son, that blood all-powerful to make atonement, for which inevitably the Father seeks a reckoning. The Father, O evil generation, stands ready to demand recompense at your hands for the blood of his Son. For you are about to put his only Son to death and to assail his powers of endurance in every way you can. Yet you will not be successful, for 'not a bone of his shall be broken.'* *Cf. Gen 1:1* *Cf. Ex 31:9* *Cf. Is 1:4* *Cf. Mt 23:35* *Jn 19:36*

3. The glorious fidelity of the martyrs, which they borrowed from the divine strength of this 'bone', is celebrated joyously in the psalm: 'The Lord keeps all their bones, not one of them is broken.'* On the other hand, the weak declare with feeble groans, 'While my bones are broken, my oppressors taunt me.'* Yet to the only Son of God belong the words quietly whispered in his Father's ear, 'My bone was not hidden from you when you *Ps 34:20* *Ps 42:12*

fashioned me in secret.'* Hence it can be seen what is portended by the death of the thieves, in that their legs were broken, and they did at once.* For we know well who used these words: 'By your endurance you will win your lives.'* Obviously, if your your life is to be won by endurance, when endurance collapses, how could life not die? So of him, who will win his life by the greatest endurance possible, and on that account should not have died this kind of death, it is truly said, 'Not a bone of his shall be broken.'* It is as if, Moses were saying: It is impossible for you, O evil nation, whatever the opportunity, whatever your exertion, to impair the firmness of his patience, in other words, to break the legs of the Son of God.

 I shall now hold my peace, but I am sure that anyone who listens will observe how beautifully and becomingly and without wounding her modesty, the bride of Jesus has succeeded in exalting with praise the legs of her beloved. But I think it is now also clear why she has spoken of them as 'columns'.

 4. For the legs of Jesus, that is, his patience and longsuffering, are truly 'columns', resting on everlasting and changeless strength. They are 'alabaster columns', because they are strong, stable, beautiful and, finally, of very great worth. They are columns upon which the whole round world and all that is in it, is supported. Not only the world, but without doubt heaven, too, leans upon these same columns, for it trembles and quakes at the good pleasure of Jesus. In short, any house not founded on these columns must of

necessity fall.* This is why the house of Israel fell, and further will not rise again* until it learns to take these columns for its foundation.

5. But oh, how long, Zion, more truly called unhappy daughter of Babylon, how long will you still be hard of heart?* How long will you refuse to be healed? How long will the wound and sore and swelling bruise of your stubborn envy and hopeless defiance* ruthlessly thrust off and loathe any remedy that will save you? Look at the hands of Jesus, which you impiously stretched out on the cross, and which to this very day are lovingly stretched out towards you. No one will turn away from it! The hand of the Lord is truly stretched out, and who will turn it away?'* Not even your very madness, which has made you curse and blaspheme him from that day to this—and in the doing strike every tribe and family among you with one great wound—not even that has taken down or will take down his extended hand. He was fastened to the cross and his words stand fast, too. 'All day long I stretched out my hands to a people who did not believe and who spoke against me.'* And in the end so long a patience will not fail to accomplish the due result.

It will came to pass, O daughter of Zion, that the Lord will take away the veil from your face,* he will bind up your wound and cover up the scar of your disfigurement. It will come, I say, that you seize the hand of the Lord, stretched out to you for so long a time, that you lay hold of it and kiss it lovingly. On

Cf. Mt 7:24
Cf. Ps 41:8

Cf. Is 47:1

Is 1:6

Cf. Is 14:27

Is 65:2

Cf. 2 Cor 3:16

that day you will indeed strike (yourself) and you will pierce through the side of Jesus, just as you do today, but in a manner wholly different. No wonder, for today he who is pierced is not seen. But of that day it is said: 'They shall look on him whom they have pierced.'* So you will see him whom you have opened wide your mouths to accuse,* whom you have nailed to the cross, at whom you have tossed your head in mockery,* whom you pierced through when he was dead. You will see him whom you shut away in a tomb and whom, now risen to new life, you too with renewed fury persecute. You will see how even as he sits in heaven, you crucify him, even to the present moment, so far as you, and every tribe and family are able.

Zech 12:10
Cf. Ps 35:21

Cf. Mk 15:29

On the day that is coming there will again be a spear in your hand, but a spear of the most piercing sorrow, to strike right through your heart and wound the heart of Jesus. You will make for yourself a great and unmistakable doorway into the side of our holy Ark, and you will enter deep within him with all your energy.* I say it again, you will batter with all your strength, you will even force your way in with violence, until the door of eternal tenderness lies open before you. Then you will go deep inside, right up to the very heart of Jesus. From the side of Jesus there will pour forth for you the blood you once sold: the same blood which bought you back anew. On that day you will be wholly bought back from the past wickedness by that blood, you will be sprinkled all over, totally washed and purified. Moreover, you will drink of it

Cf. Gen 6:16

Sermon Thirty

and be inebriated, even to the extent of almost ceasing to grieve on that day or to feel shame at having yourself been the one to shed that sacred blood.

'For the Lord will comfort Zion, he will comfort all her waste places.'* He will give you 'the oil of gladness instead of mourning, a garland instead of ashes, and the mantle of praise instead of the spirit of grief.'* Yes, on that day Joseph will comfort his brothers, so that instead of perhaps feeling ashamed to stand before him, they may rather see him and recognize him and be flooded with an indescribable joy.* He will in fact suggest, in his own brotherly and ineffable way, that all these things happened by God's will, and that what it says in scripture about the redemption of mankind could not have been fulfilled in any other manner. And then, to give them every possible comfort, he will set before them that their sin has enriched the world and that, as the apostle says, in their rejection the world is reconciled.* But now their long years of desertion will make perfect restitution and, as Isaiah says, 'the destruction will be cut short and will overflow with holiness.'*

Is 51:3
Is 61:3
Cf. Gen 45:5,8
Cf. Rom 11:15
Is 10:22

Therefore the day will come when it will be clearly seen that charity is the foundation and the ground of this whole affair, and then will be fulfilled what the bride sings in those words of praise that we are now discussing: 'His legs are alabaster columns, set in sockets of pure gold.'* For the verdict of God's love is truly set in a golden and unchangeable socket, decreeing in his eternal plan that there

Sg 5:15

should be a rebuilding of the ruined house of Israel.

6. But there is another golden socket upon which the column of the divine patience also stands. Set in this socket it bore with great endurance the blindness of all nations, right up to the last days. Now, however, in the fulness of the time, when his plan was ready, God has turned the blindness of Israel into the light of the nations. So the ruin of both Israel and the nations may become the salvation of them both, the first cause that lies behind all other causes, and their supreme fulfillment, may be love.

It follows, then, that the bride of Christ, (and by bride I mean her, who has been raised up from the nations to the dignity of being married to the Only-begotten of the Father 'in genuine faith and sincere charity,'*) it follows that the bride has copious matter for joy and praise in this twofold patience and love of her spouse. So much so that her swelling heart breaks forth into a cry of praise: Truly the legs of my beloved are the strong bones of his patience and long endurance, bones, concealed by the Father of lights, bones which the Father has set up to be the columns of heaven and earth. Upon these changeless celestial supports, he has erected the whole fabric of all that he has made. And now the Spirit of charity, which my beloved bestowed on me, makes me feel compassion for the daughter of Zion. I pity her for giving my spouse a bill of divorce, that impudent and defiant step which she herself deliberately took in days gone by. But

2 Cor 6:6

I rejoice with her to the full now that we see the day coming when that bill will be torn up. And the former bond will be renewed, as it was in the days of her youth,* a new bond, 'which shall stand firm for ever.'*

Cf. Ez 16:60
Dan 2:44

When that day comes, I too shall go to meet her with exulting heart. I shall be there as a go-between to bring about a holy kiss, and in everything connected with her marriage bond I shall offer my help and mediation and testimony. It will be my delight to be present at that marriage, where I trust that I too, shall be inebriated to the last degree of joy. For at that marriage will be present my Lord Jesus, and for the nuptial day his cellars will be filled with wine.* Meanwhile I am full of joy on my own account, also, body and soul, because in divorcing his first bride, the Lord my God remembered me.

Cf. Jn 2:11

How does it happen that on me, an Ethiopian maid,* so great a Lord should bend his gaze, so tender and so unexpected? I am utterly unworthy to untie the latchet of his shoe,* oh, not even fit to wash the feet of his very servants. What am I but a daughter of Pharaoh, a servant of false gods, a handmaid of evildoers, the devils' concubine? Was not my father's house a house of hell, and is not this his inheritance, and mine too? How can this new title be mine, and such great grace and mercy come suddenly down from heaven into my bosom, beyond all expectation? And in addition, as a crowning grace, the former wife's divorce has meant that I, all unworthy and of lowly birth, have been raised to the dignity of her title and

Cf. Sg 1:6

Cf. Mk 1:7

position. So what draws this new honor is not just my own longstanding unworthiness, but the worth in days gone by of the former bride, as well as the spouse's unaccustomed and unappeasable anger against her. His ardor turns away from her so that love may flare up in me. He drives away his cousin, the nobility of whose family is beyond question, he casts off her nieces, all that he may cleave to me, a foreigner and an object of contempt.

So she has been left widowed and forsaken, and I have entered without warning into her inheritance and her marriage-bed, to reap what I have not sown, and to gather what she, not I, has scattered.* What can I do to make some response, not wholly disproportionate to his greatness, in face of this stupendous honor? For my Lord himself has actually given up his home and withdrawn from all his Jewish kinsfolk their inheritance, in order to be united with me, a woman of unclean race. What could be imagined more impressive, more noble, more passionate than this love, where solely for love of me, every other love is abandoned and outlawed? Why do I not concentrate on him all the affections of my heart, no matter what they are, no matter how great they are? He gave up everything that was his for me.

Not only has my spouse freely handed over to my authority all the graces of his previous bride, but all that she did wrong has become for me a means of salvation. It was she who shed the blood of my Lord, and it is I who bathe in it and am cleansed. She provided the cross, in which I have been given the

Cf. Mt 25:26

privilege of finding my glory.* It was she who brought about the cruel death through which I now live, and yet it is not I who live.* It was she who opened the side of my Lord, when he was dead, but it is I who have entered therein. She made for me a way of life into that inner, secret hiding place of the heart of Jesus.

Cf. Gal 6:14

Cf. Gal 2:20

There, from the side of my sleeping Lord, I have been fashioned,* for it was only to bring me into being that he chose to fall asleep. For it was not his Jewish bride who cast him into slumber. It was rather my Lord's own Father who closed his Son's eyelids in sleep,* and of his own free will he slept and took his rest.* So in that sleep it was his good pleasure that I should come forth, bone of his bone and flesh of his flesh.* And for the rest, what else remains for me but to be wholly his? For he breathed his own Spirit into me, so that there should remain within me nothing that came only from me myself.

Cf. Gen 2:21

Cf. Ps 132:4
Cf. Gen 2:23

Cf. Eph 5:30

7. In fine, fashioned wholly out of him and by him, I was brought up to him by the Father of mercies, so that he who had bestowed all these other gifts upon me, might not fail to add the glory of his name. Therefore he gave me a new name, a title which his own mouth pronounced.*

Cf. Is 61:2

But as for me, I have not yet been granted the grace of understanding the dignity of this title. No one knows that until he has received it.* However, by his grace, I shall grasp the full significance of this name when the day of my marriage arrives, and 'the bridegroom

Cf. Rev 2:17

Is 62:5   rejoices over the bride,'* and the bride likewise enters into the eternal enjoyment of her spouse, for this is his good pleasure.

May we too be made partakers of this nuptial joy by the spouse of the church, our Lord Jesus Christ, who with God the Father and the Holy Spirit lives and reigns,
God, for ever and ever.
Amen.

SERMON THIRTY-ONE

The beginning of the thirty-first sermon. Of the impious celebration of the Passover, in which the Jews immolate Christ even to this day, and of the manner of this immolation. Here, too, there is a brief summary of how the Lamb must be eaten to be pleasing to God.

I CANNOT CONCEAL from you, brethren, something that my soul conceived from the seed of what was said yesterday, and has this very night brought to birth. For we read in scripture, 'The seed is the word of God.'* Yet no one need marvel that it has all happened so quickly. Jesus was here, and he gave his blessing. Come, and if you find the harvest ripe, and reap so that 'he who sows may rejoice with him who reaps!'* As I was saying, those words of Moses, 'not a bone of his shall be broken,'* seem to me to have given rise to a rich harvest of meaning. For that great man, faithful, as scripture says, 'in all that concerns God's house',* seems to me, by the wonderful artistry of the Holy Spirit, to have sung, at one and the same time, a song of marriage to his beloved and a song of mourning to the house of Israel.

2. By bringing before the sons of Israel the figure of the paschal lamb, and by bringing God's people out of the land of

Lk 8:11

Jn 4:36

Jn 19:36

Cf. 1 Sam 22:14

Egypt in his blood,* he pointed straight at the only Son of the Father, as if with a stabbing finger, and said, 'See, here is the Lamb of God, here is he who takes away the sins of the world.'* Here is he for whom 'my heart breaks into a song of praise,'* so that at the beginning of my book, it is of him that I write.* He is that greatest and eternal 'beginning', in which God made heaven and earth,* he is the Word of the Father, for he spoke, and all was made.* Whatever I have written, it is he whom I was writing about, telling and declaring all my works to the king.* Finally, when I bent in adoration, and kept on repeating, 'Lord, if I have found grace in your sight,* show me your face,'† then it was his face that I longed to see with a longing past description.

I have been lifted out of myself, but God has not let me down.* For I have seen 'the day of Jesus', I have seen it and been filled with joy.* I have seen the one I long for, I have seen the one I wait for, I have seen the light of my eyes, I have seen the king in his splendor and the beautiful one in his beauty. I have seen him in his glory on the mountain, I have seen 'him face to face, and yet my life has been preserved.'* And then, on that day, not only was there a new light shining in my eyes, but even my ears, too, knew joy, pealing in thunderous rapture from the heavens! For the Father, 'faithful witness in the heavens,'* bore witness to his Son for me to hear, so that from that day forth, blessed have been my eyes, and blessed, too, my ears!*

After all this, how joyfully I came down from the mountain, how much more joyfully than once I came down from Mount Sinai! I came down with my face shining with a glory greater than I had ever known, for on it was impressed the glory and splendor of the wonderful light that streams from the face of Jesus. So I returned to the true sons of Israel, to those who rest upon Abraham's bosom, waiting to see what I saw. And I gave them 'good tidings of great joy',* because I looked upon the glory of the Son of God.

Cf. Lk 2:10

See, his glory is at our very threshold! The time has come for the Lamb to be led to the slaughter. Already the sons of Israel are making plans to slay him, already every house and family is arranging to consume him. Stand firm, then, because tomorrow, in the blood of this Lamb,* we shall escape from this captivity.† Tomorrow is the true Passover, when Christ our passover will be sacrificed, and we ourselves shall celebrate it with him.*

*Cf. Responsory from first nocturn of The Vigils of Christmas Eve.
†Cf. Ex 12:27

Cf. 1 Cor 5:7

3. But what unhappiness is yours, you evil and faithless people, who keep the passover feast by killing the spotless Lamb of God!* Oh, how unhappy, for every tribe and family among you has plotted together to this end, and you have transmitted the inherited observance of this wickedness from one generation to the next! What made you become so stubborn in your impiety? What evil has he done? Or rather, what good has he not done? What has he not done to help you? The Lamb of God is quite certainly 'without blemish', he is 'a male', he is 'a year old'.* Which of

Cf. 1 P 1:19, Heb 9:14

Cf. Ex 12:5

you can accuse him of sin?* Into the virgin's son, 'nothing defiled gains entrance.'* Indeed, he was born, he came into the world, for this very purpose,* that in him evildoing might receive its deathblow.

So then he is 'without blemish', and furthermore, he is 'a male', in case he be thought able to be deceived by woman's folly, or seduced by her weakness. He is totally free of that muddled thinking by which a woman brought about original sin, so that Eve could say, 'The serpent deceived me.' And he is free, too, of Adam's softness of fibre, which had been made womanish through a woman, so that Adam could say, 'The woman deceived me.'* In both respects, our Lamb is a male, and he can neither be deceived nor weakened in that way. Furthermore, I have spoken of him as 'a yearling', praising his exceptional strength, which makes him the only one able to defend the flock constantly, and also make it fruitful. It is his strength that protects the sheep of God's pasture and his grace that makes them bear fruit. It is, in fact, the Lamb who both guards the sheep and brings the lambs to birth.

So this Lamb possesses perfect innocence, because he is without blemish, perfect wisdom, because he is a male, perfect strength and universal grace, because he is a yearling.

What if his fleece were looked at by loving eyes and fingered by pure hands? And his flesh, what if it should be tasted and appreciated by a healthy palate, though not by a sickly? What if his blood should find a pure throat, which would savor it for what it is?

Margin notes:
Cf. Jn 8:46
Cf. Wis 7:25
Cf. Jn 18:37
Gen 3:12, 13

At any rate, this is the whitest and softest fleece, the tenderest and richest flesh, while his blood is blood of the finest grapes, wine of the choicest stock.* So the fleece of this Lamb is gentle lowliness; his flesh is tender kindness; his blood is holy delight. His fleece is truly a mantle, his flesh is truly food, and his blood is truly drink.* Whoever covers himself with this fleece, will not fear the coming of winter cold,* or the shame of being naked. Whoever makes his meal on this flesh, will not dread hunger or disease. Whoever drinks this blood, will not thirst or grow sad for all eternity.*

Cf. Deut 32:14

Cf. Jn 6:54

Cf. Ps 147:17

Cf. Jn 6:54

This is the true keeping of the Passover: piously to eat this flesh and drink this blood, and so become incorporated into this Lamb, and in this way, actually become the Lamb.

4. But oh, wretched house of Israel, you have turned yourself into a wolf as regards this Lamb! For like a wolf breathing and panting out threats of slaughter,* like an evening wolf you have waited until evening to break forth out of your ambush. The sheep have fled in fear, and like a wolf, you rush upon the Lamb, tearing his fleece to pieces, fiercely rending his flesh, shedding his blood. And then not like men but like beasts, your ritual demands you consume the head and the feet and the entrails, and you leave nothing of him until morning.* Yet after this total consumption, O house of Israel, you still remain famished and the Lamb still remains untouched and whole. And in very truth these things were done 'in the evening', because your sun has set. It has set upon your

Cf. Acts 9:1

Cf. Ex 12:9, 10

implacable anger, upon your insane hatred, upon your incurable blindness. Amazingly, your sun set at full moon, when the Sun was shining in all his strength, radiant in your midst with his words of grace and his signs of glory.

You were impious in committing sacrilege, and you were just as obstinate in alleging excuses for it. You built for yourself a door by which in the future the Lamb could not enter. For it is clear that the door, by which Jesus comes to sinners, has each of these doorposts on either side, holy fear and loving sorrow, while the lintel is a pure sense of shame. But upon each of these doorposts, and on that lintel, is the blood of the sinless Lamb.* Anyone who looks upon it with love, as he goes into the house of his conscience through secret remorse, or as he goes out of that house through humble confession, immediately draws fresh breath in the confidence of forgiveness, since he ponders on the price of his redemption.

Cf. Ex 12:7

But how tragic is your lot, house of Israel! You have set up in your heart, like twin doorposts, a complete refusal to feel fear or sorrow at the shedding of such great blood, and for a lintel, you have laid down a defiant rejection of the sense of shame. The two posts of your doorway are rash over-confidence and impenitent obstinacy, and your lintel is not unlike them, a bold shamelessness and a stubborn impudence. What wonder, if Jesus leaves your house deserted, if he passes through it, leaving no blessing behind him, especially since he sees the doorway of this house stained with his blood in these three ways?* Yet even to this day, the blood of his only Son cries out to the Father from the gateway of this house. There is nowhere for the sons of Israel to turn aside, they cannot go in or go out, without this blood forcing itself upon their attention, their accuser and their judge, but also their deliverer. *Cf. Mt 23:38*

5. There is something awesome about a wickedness that neither feared the Lord Jesus as God, nor respected him as man. When the Jews accused him to Pilate, on the grounds that he 'made himself the Son of God',* Pilate, at all events, was thunderstruck at hearing 'Son of God', and was overcome by a very righteous fear. Then, too, the humility and silence of Jesus before the great injustice of his accusers, made Pilate 'wonder very much', the gospel tells us.* But as for you, with your insatiable greed you devour his head together with his feet and entrails,* the majesty of such great dignity does not frighten you nor the humility of such great majesty affect you nor the goodness of such tender mercy touch you. If your envy fastened on his pre-eminence surely it might have exempted his suffering, or at least, his mercy? But in one great gulp, O unhappy people, you swallowed down the whole of him, and you did not stop to wonder. And when Pilate wondered and pitied and feared, you swallowed him down too, with the same arrogant self-confidence, so that, having swallowed him, you might more readily absorb Jesus through him. *Cf. Jn 19:7* *Cf. Mk 15:5* *Cf. Ex 12:9*

So there is nothing at all in our Lamb that

the fire of your burning has not broiled.* You have seen to it that there is nothing in him that is raw or boiled, but only what has been roasted in the fire. For if you had gone outside the bounds of the law to lay your wicked hands on him, or not searched high and low for an official judge, then you would have devoured him 'raw'. Again, if you had destroyed him after making him endure a long drawn out but less painful agony, you would have eaten him, as it were, 'cooked in water', where there is a milder flame. But as it is, as a cloak for your impiety, you resort to a trial the law lays down, as if to cover up your crime with an appearance of judicial impartiality—and you are all the more wicked for your dishonesty! You could not even suffer a delay, but, all eagerness to shed his blood, you begged earnestly for him to be tormented with the anguish of the cross and not a milder pain that would destroy him little by little. Moreover, besides the bodily torture, there would be the sheer disgrace of the cross to burn him up with a fierce heat.

6. And so from that day, or rather, from that night, from then on, in fact, night took hold of you, and you have walked blindly in the darkness ever since. From then on, the Lord broke the 'staff of bread' in Jerusalem,* because all the unleavened bread tastes of Jesus,* and you have made it tasteless and of no avail with your wild lettuce, that is, with your wild and ridiculous interpretation. It is a well established fact that all the bread of doctrine, of whatever kind, however fresh it is, however rich, if it does not taste of the

Sermon Thirty-One

wisdom of God, which is Christ, has either no flavor at all, or at least, has not the flavor that it ought to have.

But you, into whose keeping were given the inspired words of God, which on every page press Jesus on your attention, which continually and with one voice accuse you of impiety, what excuse have you to be let remain among men of wise and discriminating taste? Your heart is gross indeed,* not so much struggling to endure the great denseness of its ignorance, but actually going out of its way to cherish it. Then, you have cleverly taken steps about your unhappy state and done all you can to protect yourself and your children in the future, in case any spark of truth be coaxed from the holy scriptures and the light of faith burst into flame. You have taken careful precautions for yourself and your offspring, in case, after the long and gloomy night of your blindness, someone may strike his heart and rise early in the morning to watch for the true light, which is Christ.* You have laid a cruel curse on your own seed, your evil seed, involving them too in the guilt of this blood,* so much so, that for them also, 'there will be nothing left' of Jesus when day breaks.*

Was your impiety so violent that it looked for destruction and even more, so that it could not endure to be suspended by the cross of Christ, could not die when he was dead, could not rest when he was buried? You hounded him from prison to the judgement seat, from the judgement seat to the scourging, from the scourging to the cross,

Cf. Mt 13:15

Cf. Jn 9:5

Cf. Mt 27:25

Cf. Ex 12:10

from the cross to the tomb. Do you think even there the Lord Jesus may find himself at peace? A new and hitherto unheard of form of militia or rather malice: to ring a fort such as that with an armed guard.* But to what purpose? Clearly so that nothing of Jesus should remain 'till the morning',* and that all hope of his resurrection be buried with him in the depth of the tomb.

But what in the end was the result of this band of soldiers? In a new and altogether unheard of fashion, they precisely frustrated their original purpose! By your act of impiety, you yourself made public the glory of the resurrection! For us, indeed, it was our life and resurrection that rose from the dead, but for you, oh unhappy sons of Israel, Christ is still buried, still crucified, your life still hangs before your eyes in doubt.*

In all this, you have one sole comfort for your blindness, the testimony of your conscience.* You claim that you are zealous for God, and that you are eager to follow the traditions of your fathers. Therefore you prepare to eat the passover lamb by girding your loins with the belt of this so-called virtue, your feet shod with the authority of misapplied models.* But nevertheless, this loincloth is completely decayed, and these shoes are to no purpose. Virtue is by all means the girdle for the loins,* but it must come from faith, it must be in accordance with knowledge. Otherwise, except when faith too, supports our virtue like a girdle, virtue itself becomes unvirtuous.

In general, you are very ready for battle,

holding sticks in your hands, on the alert to give an answer to all who ask the reason for the lack of faith that is in you.* All who would pity you, who try to call you back to Christ and strive to bring you once again into friendship with him, you drive away with your stick, as if resisting a wolf, and you raise your stick against them in furious attack. Therefore your wound is in every way hopeless, and for the time being, it is deliberately left uncured, because of the danger that the very cure may make it all the more incurable.* *Cf. 1 Pet 3:15*

Cf. Mich 1:9

7. This is why the healer says despairingly, 'My jealous love has withdrawn from you, I shall do longer be angry with you.'* The same thing is obviously being said, in other words, when he says, 'You shall eat it in haste, for it is the Passover, that is, the passing of the Lord.'* 'You shall eat it,' he says, 'in haste,' namely, putting no question to yourselves, but making an empty boast of 'the testimony of your conscience'. The result is that the closer you are to your boasting, the further you are from your healing. So, as the healer passes along, no way of approach to the sick lies open, any avenue of bringing him sympathy is blocked, all paths that would lead to his cure are thickly overgrown. In consequence, Jesus passes by, because he does not turn his eyes towards sickly Israel; he passes by, because there is no one to rise up and catch hold of him.* He passes by and does not yet stand still, because up to the present, nothing is seen in him except only his manhood and his death, the light of his eternity is invisible.

Cf. Ez 16:42

Ex 12:11

Cf. Is 64:7

But at the end of time, he will stop and stand, for then he will hear the blind crying out, 'Have mercy on me, son of David!'* Here and now, there is no one able to be healed, supposing by chance there be anyone out of all the children whom the unhappy daughter of Zion has nourished, who even wanted to be healed. There is no one to notice the man wounded by the robbers, no priest, no levite, and up to this very day, not even a Samaritan.* All pass by. The Samaritan too passes by. 'This is the Passover, that is, the passing of the Lord.'*

8. 'But oh Lord, how long will you wait?'* 'Are we not right to say of you that you are a Samaritan,'* for you have treated us with mercy and you have bound up our wounds? How long, I repeat, will you pass along with your eyes shut, making believe not to see, keeping your mind closed, passing unnoticed, fleeing away, suppressing your tenderness, hardening your heart? This wound is so desperate and so long lasting; 'O, merciful and compassionate Lord,'* but surely you have healing for it? Look upon your covenant,* and 'do not break the agreement'† which you have sealed, which you have sworn, which you have put in writing, which you have signed. Lord God of our salvation, Lord Jesus, show that 'Jesus' means 'savior', by this wonderful act of your saving power! 'Reveal the marvels of your mercy,'* so that you outdo the greatness of that sinfulness by the greatness of your tender pity! It is true that 'from the sole of her foot to the crown of her head, there is no health in her,'* yet we

know for ourselves what the touch of your compassion can do, that if you but touch her, she will immediately be set free.* Then, lay your hand upon her, that, at its blessed touch, virtue may go out of you and health come forth,* to the praise and glory of your name, you who with God the Father
and the Holy Spirit,
live and reign,
God, for ever
and ever.
Amen.

Cf. Lk 8:47

Cf. Lk 8:46

SERMON THIRTY-TWO

The beginning of the thirty-second sermon. Of the right and holy celebration of the Passover, in which the sons of Israel will immolate the Lamb, as well as their manner of keeping the Passover at the time of their final conversion.

WHAT YOUR TENDER MERCY has in store for the house of Israel, O loving Lord, Father of mercies,* is hidden within your breast. The time of your good pleasure, the time when you take compassion on it,* you know when it is, and you have it safely laid up in your treasuries. It is you who have control of it, and so it is something absolutely certain. From nowhere but those treasuries of yours came that tender and repeated prayer found in the heart and on the lips of your prophets, and deeply impressed by them on your gracious ears: 'Remember your own people who have been your possession from the beginning.'* And, 'how long, Lord, will you have no mercy on what is left of Jerusalem?'* And again: 'Return for the sake of your servants, the tribes of your inheritance!'* Therefore, 'look down from heaven and see, visit your vine, and perfect what your right hand has planted.'* Then, Lord God, send forth, in

Cf. Ps 69:14

Cf. Ps 102:13

Ps 74:2

Cf. Zech 1:12

Is 63:17

Ps 80:14-15

Sermon Thirty-Two

answer to your servants' prayer, send forth the Lamb of your gentleness, who is already lord and king over all the earth! Send him forth 'from the rock of the desert,' from the faith of all peoples, 'to the mount of the daughter of Zion.'* *Cf. Is 11:6*

You are so great, Lord; do something the earth has never seen before; make the wolf dwell with the lamb, in peace and innocence, and the lamb with the wolf, in trustful freedom!* This is certainly the miraculous sign for which the children of Israel admit they are waiting, considering it as incontroveritable evidence of the coming of the Messiah whom they are expecting. Then, Lord, make the whole world and all that is in it, stand aghast, as scripture says,* and make the wolf and the lamb come before you to conclude a new alliance. Let the lamb agree to have no fear of being eaten by the wolf, and the wolf harbor no suspicion of the lamb. Let the wolf share his home with the lamb, and from sharing the lamb's home, let him share the lamb's nature. By all means, let him eat, but with new teeth, with innocent simplicity and simple innocence.* *Cf. Is 65:25*

Cf. Is 41:5

Cf. Is 65:25

When that time comes, the house of Israel will keep a new and solemn Passover. They will inaugurate a day of solemn festival* with branches in their hands, and they will summon the whole assembly of the children of Israel to celebrate the Lord's Passover* with new rites, in its true and proper observance. Nor, as pious belief has it, will a single one be missing out of all the great crowd of every tribe and family of Israel, *Cf. Ps 118:27*

Cf. Ex 12:47

not one who will not hasten to the solemn festival. The whole throng of the sons of Israel will come before the Lord to sacrifice the Lamb of their age-old sacrifice, doing penance although late in the day, and then reaping a harvest once more because of their penitence. The tardier that repentance, the bitter; and the later, the more likely to be heartfelt. So this sacrifice will take place when the world's sun is going down, and as they make it, they will mourn that they have come so late, and yet they will rejoice that they came before the utter darkness of pitch-black night.

O good Jesus, when Israel realizes the dread presence of the Lord, and the glory of his majesty, what floods of tears will burst forth at seeing how impiously and cruelly they once immolated this Lamb? It is indisputably clear, that among all the sorrows that repentance can experience, there has never been and there will never be in time to come, anything like this sorrow or comparable to these tears.* As the prophet says, they will beat their breast, family by family; and they will beat it in mourning for the Son of God, lamenting as one laments for the death of the first-born.* Lord God, is there any order to these lamentations, and, amid such a turmoil of sighing, can this great multitude of sighs be clearly distinguished one from another?

So on each of their doorposts, and on the threshold, Israel will put the mark of this precious blood, and in three ways they will make themselves suffer in reparation for its shedding. For Israel will be seized with an

Cf. Lam 1:12

Cf. Zech 12:12

overwhelming fear and will be filled with immense grief and will be most bitterly ashamed. The life of Israel will 'hang in doubt' before their eyes,* whenever they go in or go out of their dwelling-place; that is, interiorly they will afflict themselves with remorse, and exteriorly with lamentation. Wherever Israel goes, his mind will be preoccupied with the hand of the crucified, stretched out above him, and there is no means of avoiding it. The only possibility of escape is to 'enter into the rock',* searching deep sighs of contrition, followed in time by the effects [proper] to contrition, it too, hollowed out of the earth of Jesus' breast. Consequently, Israel will be marking the entire length and breadth of his gates with the very blood he has spilt with his own hand. He will indeed tremble prodigiously with dread at the weight of his beloved, but he will also weigh what he has cost that beloved, faithfully repay it, tenderly marvel at it, and confidently take it to himself.

Cf. Deut 28:66

Cf. Sg 2:14

2. With assurance, then, Israel will approach to the throne of the grace of Jesus,* where it may religiously reap what it irreligiously sowed,* and where the blood it spilt, not knowing what it did,* it may now drink, knowing well what it does.* After such deep sighs of contrition, followed in time by the effects (proper) to contrition, it too, will at last approach, as if with hands washed and purified, to sit down at Jesus' table. The flesh of the Lamb will be laid before it, but now roasted in a new fire, the love of Jesus, which will have to be sent down from

Cf. Heb 4:16

Cf. Ps 126:6
Cf. Lk 23:34
Cf. 1 Cor 11:28

heaven. What will keep that fire going, and powerfully enkindle it, is that dense woodland of trouble and bitterness which, to its present wonder, it once inflicted on the Son of God in its mental blindness.

Also at that table, Israel will have the happiness of being served with unleavened bread, when Jesus, opening his mouth, opens to them their mind and, in the light of the gospel, explains Moses and the prophets.* *Cf. Lk 34:27.* Then all the leaven of malice and evil, which is now within the Jewish heart, will be cast out of the house.* *Cf. 1 Cor 5:8* From that time on, Israel, its own face equally unveiled, will behold the face of Moses, for, without any doubt, it will be granted to behold the glory of the face of Jesus.* *Cf. Ex 34:33* So the face of neither will be concealed from the other, and by that twofold grace, Israel 'will see light in light'.* *Cf. Ps 36:9*

Hence, Israel will eat 'unleavened bread and with it, bitter herbs.'* *Ex 12:8* Bringing together, with gospel simplicity, whatever has been prophesied concerning Jesus, in many different places and ways, it will, as it were, make the sublimity of the words of God savory and healthy for itself, with the bitter and lowly savor of the lowliness of Christ. For in a wonderful way, sublimity appears more agreeable when seasoned with lowliness, and while losing none of its integrity, it tastes sweeter to the mouth. Yet this pleasure is hidden from the wise and learned, and only to the uncultured, that is to little ones, is it revealed.* *Cf. Mt 11:25* Up to this, Israel ignored this bitter, uncultivated flavor, and sought only after God's sublimity, scorning lowliness. So,

Sermon Thirty-Two

as the apostle says, 'what Israel sought it failed to obtain,'* and what it did not seek, it obviously did not lay hold on.*

Rom 11:7
Cf. Phil 3:12

3. But when they return to the Lord, Israel will taste with clean throat the incarnate Wisdom of God. It will season his greatness with lowliness and his lowliness with sublimity. It will joyfully perceive with power 'the weakness of God', and it will sweetly savor with wisdom 'the foolishness of God.'* Accustomed now to this gladness, it will eat the head, not only with the feet, but even with the entrails, so as to season the eternal majesty of the Lord Jesus by no means only with the most reverent humility, but also with the most delightful intimacy. So Israel will search deep into the depths of the heart of Jesus, and with that very rich tissue which surrounds that sacred organ, it will enrich its own heart. Besides, love, being very eager and ravenous, will not easily be able to hold itself back at that banquet and be checked by the reins of moderation, all the more because their conversion has been late in the day. So, as scripture says, 'they will suffer hunger, like dogs'.* And the more Israel eats, so much the more will it hunger, so that in those days it will be as if the Lamb said to them: 'Those who eat me, will yet feel hunger.'* Yet Moses does not say that they are to eat, but that they are to devour, making it quite clear that the hunger of Israel is wholly insatiable, and that no hope of satisfying it will ever dawn until the glory of the Lord Jesus becomes visible.

1 Cor 1:25

Ps 59:6

Sir 24:21

4. Furthermore, in keeping the Passover,

there are two things in particular which are strictly forbidden: that it is not to be eaten raw or cooked in water.* Now to eat the Lamb raw means to be sluggish and cold, lacking the fire of charity, to glory in the holy name of Christ in vain. But to do the cooking in water means to plunge the tenderness of faith into carnal desires. If anyone is without love for God and for his brother, and gives himself to wrangling and envy, then he either does not eat the Lamb at all, or he eats it raw, that is, red with the blood of his own sinfulness. While anyone who has not yet raised himself out of the waters of carnal desires, buoys up but an empty self-esteem by the tenderness of his faith or the holiness of his religion.

Cf. Ex 12:9

But far from the sons of Israel be both these evils, for on that day, as Isaiah says, the remnant of Israel will come back to the Lord in truth.* In proportion to the enormity of their sin will be the measure of tears assigned them, and this measure will be counterbalanced by the size of their love. The reality of that conversion will surely be so great, so great its completeness, that they will be a sign and an example to the whole Church of believers.

Cf. Is 10:21

Therefore, they will leave nothing of the Lamb over until morning,* as our wretched tepidity would wish, so as to rely proudly on tomorrow and take no trouble for today. Salvation through repentance is late and uncertain, and it is the height of rash folly to do what requires reparation in the hope of being able to make that reparation.

Cf. Ex 12:10

Do not, if you are wise, depend upon tomorrow; whatever your hand is able to do, do it this very minute, with no delay,* and then nothing of the Lamb's flesh will remain until the morning. And yet, human nature being what it is, if something were to be secretly withheld, so that there would be in a sense, something remaining, this remnant too the fire of love would consume with a sigh of repentance.   *Cf. Qo 9:10*

5. But Moses has yet more to say to that assembly of the children of Israel on whom that blessed day will dawn. 'This is how you are to eat the Lamb. You will gird your loins, you will have shoes on your feet, you will hold staffs in your hands, and you will eat in haste.'*   *Ex 12:11*

On that day the house of Israel will indeed be girt with a new loin cloth, one that the flower of Jesse's root bound around himself. 'The girdle of his loins', he says, 'will be holiness, and faith will be girt around his thighs.'* Long before that day, the old girdle, holiness according to the law, had rotted and fallen apart. Instead of putting concupiscence to death, it rather, as the apostle remarks, made it grow, increasing beyond all measure.* But the girdle of the holiness of faith is utterly trustworthy and indestructible, binding the loins with chastity as well as consecrating the heart's purity. So the whole house of Israel will be girt at the same time with this loincloth. It will place its trust only in the grace of our Lord and Savior, which alone is perfect and lasting holiness.   *Cf. Is 11:1*   *Cf. Rom 7:13*

Then it will take off its old shoes, for indeed the ground on which it was standing, is holy ground, and run forward, barefooted like Moses, to see this strange sight.* And from then on, it will receive new shoes, in preparation for the gospel of peace.*

On that day, it will truly put on as a garment a zealous love for apostolic perfection and charity. As it is written, it will 'go about the city',* which means it will make compensation for all that was lost in its long years of blindness, by now giving light to many. This is why the apostle says, 'If their rejection means the reconciliation of the world, what will their full inclusion mean?* Moreover, they will not be girding themselves for this task without equipment, but they will be holding staffs in their hands. For, 'to those who preach the gospel, the Lord will give his word with great power,'* for the crushing of all impiety, for the destruction of all sinfulness, for the driving away of sinfulness. There will indeed be these staffs in their hands, for the very purpose of strengthening the word of truth by the example of their life and the effect of their virtue.

They will preach the gospel, then, and they will 'eat with haste', because with a passionate eagerness of spirit, they will pass down into their belly, that is, into the body of the church, those whom they have converted from an evil life.

6. At the end, these words are added: 'For it is the Passover, that is, the Lord's passing.'* In the profoundest sense, the true keeping of the Passover is this: first to put on

Cf. Ex 3:5

Cf. Eph 6:15

Cf. Sg 3:2

Rom 11:15

Cf. Ps 68:11

Ex 12:12

charity, which is to feed on the flesh of the Lamb, and secondly to incorporate others into Christ, as far as grace makes possible. This is indeed a good and life-saving passing of the Saviour, from which arise medicines that will cure, from which healing spreads abroad and the health of salvation becomes ours.

Finally, there is a condition laid down for eating the Lamb, a holy one and full of charity. This says that, if those who have come to eat the Lamb are too few, they are to join to themselves 'the neighbor next to their house' till there is the number of persons necessary.* The apostles acted in accord with the charity of this holy condition. They saw very clearly that Israel was not able to encompass in its entirety the grace of the glory of the Word-made-flesh, even if it all flowed together as one to receive it (and how much less, since, not wanting the grace, it cut itself off from sharing in it!). This is why the apostles set out on their holy and justified passage to the gentiles. Before that day the house of the gentiles was very far distant, yet by means of the 'cornerstone', it not only became very close, but actually touched it.* In fact, it became one with it.

On that day, therefore, there was a great and solemn celebration of the Passover, when the Lord 'passed over' from Israel to the gentiles. Nevertheless, on this glorious day still to come, there will truly be a grand and most festive Passover, for then at long last, the Lord will 'pass over' from the gentiles to Israel, and in the same way, salvation will have to spread out from Israel itself into all

Cf. Ex 12:4

Cf. Ps 118:22

the corners of the world.

7. But vainglory and pride so often undermine the highest virtues, and someone may suspect that their stain may creep in here, where there is the beauty of so much grace, and such perfection of virtue. To prevent this, at the very end, there is this addition about the end of the Passover. 'Not a bone of his shall be broken.'* As they make their meal on the Lamb, they will truly have 'broken his bone', if they take a foolish delight in the joy of the grace they see within them. Israel has broken a bone of the Lamb, if he accepts God's mercy but forgets his justice, if he does not tremble at the thought of his judgements. Israel in eating the flesh would break a bone if he lost his respect for God's judgements because of his experience of the grace which is within him, coming from and through the Lamb. Besides, there would be damage, and perhaps great danger for his life, if a broken bone, swallowed down with overcareless haste, should stick in his throat when eating, and afterwards there be no one to take it out.

Jn 19:36, cf. Ex 12:46

So then, that there be nothing wanting to the celebration of this great Passover, all will join their voices into one to sing to you, O Lord, of mercy and justice! Mercy and truth will go before your face,* linked closely together, so that the blessed people, 'who know the joyful shout',* may never fall away from that joyful shout, never falter in it, never take a false pride in it. May the grace of that joy come to us, also, grace in his truth, and truth in his grace, through the gift of

Cf. Ps 89:15

Cf. Ps 89:16

the spotless Lamb of God, spouse of the
church, Our Lord Jesus Christ, who with
God the Father and the Holy Spirit,
lives and reigns, God,
for ever and ever.
Amen.

SERMON THIRTY-THREE

Of holy fruitfulness and holy pleasure, which are what is meant by 'the thigh of the spouse'; and how the spouse is armed with a sword of fire as protection for his thigh.

Sg 5:15

'HIS LEGS ARE ALABASTER columns, set in sockets of pure gold.'* This is what the bride says. But what does David say? For he too, has a marriage song, and while he sings, he dances with all his heart before the Lord's ark.* He is singing to 'the fairest of the sons of men,'* his noble heart pouring out a noble theme,* and with sweet sounding lute and harp,* he crowns his nuptial bliss. So he tunes his instrument and praises his delight in words like these: 'Gird your sword upon your thigh, O mighty one!'*

Cf. 2 Sam 6:16
Ps 45:3
Ps 45:1
Cf. Ps 81:2

Ps 45:4

2. Whether there is really some difference between 'thigh' and 'leg', I leave as the special province of those skilled in verbal subtleties. But I am not going to concern myself with it, as I find holy scripture using both words indifferently. For our part, let us rather compare what both marriage songs have to say in praise, in the hope that this very comparison, guided by the same Spirit of love, will unfold for us the mysterious depths in the words of both.

Cf. Gen 6:3

But in speaking to me, a man of flesh,* the

Spirit sees fit to use words of flesh and of fleshly desire, gently and graciously making my desire wholesome, that he may clothe me in his. I embrace the loving condescension, I marvel at the wisdom, I give thanks for the tender mercy which once 'lowered his heavens',* when 'the Word was made flesh.'† Since I too, am flesh, it is now possible for me, even me, to draw near to him who draws near to me. I long to climb up to him 'who lives in the heavens',* and so he has set up a ladder for me, made of words like these, by which, somehow or other, I can slowly and step by step venture towards him. But I cannot climb safely up to him unless the Lord Jesus supports that ladder from above, holding it so that it does not sway. I need him, to speak to his servant's heart,* and first to send to me one of those angels of his, who go up and down upon that ladder,* so that in his hands I may be led as far along it as he sees is possible for me.

*Cf. Ps 18:9
†Jn 1:14

Cf. Ps 2:4

Cf. Ruth 2:13

Cf. Gen 28:10, RB 7.6

2. The image here is of fleshly love, and if we are to follow it chastely and prudently, we must understand what the thigh signifies. It contains the seedbed of fleshly temptation, and, at the same time, the vigor of human fruitfulness, being thus a sign both of the mysteries of sacred pleasure and of the fruit that is most chastely begotten. Certainly it would be wrong to think that this heavenly and spotless marriage was either less delightful, or lacking in fruitfulness. The great stream of holy pleasure, where will it run, or along what path, if it does not turn into that marriage chamber and fill it to the full?

Indeed, where can pleasure be, if not here? As far as 'the heavens are higher' than the earth,* or rather, as much as 'light differs from darkness,'* to the same degree does the pleasure that comes from heaven differ from that which comes from flesh and is flesh, and the fruit of the light differ from the joys of the darkness.*

Poor flesh and blood, unworthy to taste this sweetness, and so all ignorant of a hunger for it! From the heights of true delight, they flow downwards into the muddy depths, and there become so lost to reason that they say in their hearts and think in their minds that bitter is sweet and sweet bitter.* But truly happy, indeed, happiest of all women, is she who consecrates all her desires to this holy delight, who strives to remain unaware of all other sweetness because of Jesus, and who wants to know nothing, but only Jesus.* She knows well that in him is found all sweetness, or, to speak more truly, she has herself most assuredly experienced, in countless ways, that he is the well spring of all delight.

She rises, then, and walks about the 'land, flowing with milk and honey,'* the land that is Jesus himself. She walks about the length and breadth of it, as much as heavenly grace allows her. Now the taste of her spouse's sweetness comes from his kisses, and now it is in the fragrance of his ointments. At one time she knows the rapture of his embraces, at another her joy is to be with him, speaking and conversing, and yet again, she has the privilege of contemplating his beauty.* The spouse affects her in one way when he is

Is 53:9

Qo 2:3

Cf. Eph 5:9

Cf. Is 5:20

*Cf. Mk 9:8, Bernard, SC 15.6; SBOp 1:86; CF 4:109-110.

Deut 6:3

Cf. Gilbert SC 1.6; PL 184:21A: CF 14:49-50.

present, and she can enjoy him, and in quite another when he is absent and she longs for him. Sometimes she is praised by him with the most indulgent love, and sometimes it is she who wonders and praises, when the very effort to do justice to her wonderful and praiseworthy beloved, leaves her speechless.

Who can count, or even distinguish all the different ways of feeling joy, all the varieties of happiness, all the overflowing of bliss? Not even she who has been favored with their experience. A pleasure so noble and so manifold gives rise to offspring upon offspring, until the full measure of contentment has been reached.

4. The presence of Jesus is never sterile. Wherever he goes, provided only he comes in grace and not in his anger, he brings a blessing, so that 'our earth yields its fruit.'* The Word of God never returns to him empty, but 'it achieves what it was sent to do,'* and produces rich and wholly indescribable fruit. For, 'who can describe the generation'* of the Word. Obviously no one, either that generation by which he was begotten by the Father from before the ages, or that by which he was born of his mother at the end of ages. But there is another generation too, in which, with supreme graciousness, he generates sons of grace, and in those sons of grace, the gifts of grace, and no man's power can understand its manner or its effects.

5. Your charity can now consider, along with me, why the spouse thinks it fitting to gird his sword upon the thigh of such great pleasure and fruitfulness.* It is obviously

Ps 85:12

Is 55:11

Is 53:8

Cf. Ps 45:4

because that thigh is a holy place enshrining very great joy and power, and so it needs to be shielded with manly courage, guarded with care, and conscientiously kept hidden. For, 'it is a glory to hide the Word of God,'* and, as Isaiah says, 'There will be a shield over all the glory.'* Hence the most holy thigh of Jesus is shielded, sheltered from the enemies of grace, it is guarded and kept safe for his friends, it is hidden and reserved for his little ones. The foes of Jesus are driven away by the 'sword of the Spirit, which is the Word of God,'* and so they do not come near him. But his friends, on the other hand, are kept safe within, so that there is no question of their being driven off, and the little ones wait patiently on the doorstep.

The mighty one, then, binds his sword upon his thigh, most mighty, and at the same time, most beautiful.* With the two-edged sword of his love he pierces to the heart any soul that longs for Jesus and embraces the sacred delights of his pure thigh, for only then, dying to the allurements of the flesh, is it able at last to grasp and to hold what it desires. In fact, above this spiritual bliss is affixed the words: 'Many cannot see me and live.'* And also these: 'The Spirit will not abide for ever in these men, for they are flesh.'*

6. 'Therefore, gird your sword upon your thigh,'* your pure, your holy, your lovely thigh, O beautiful one, O mighty one, O infinitely desired! And then wound with your sword my thigh, my shameful thigh, with all its loathsome sores. Lord my God, cause

all the sinews of my thigh to wither* so that, *Cf. Gen 32:25*
with all my sinful lust put to sleep and put to
death by your touch, I may not be driven
away from coming near to your most holy
thigh. Gird on, I cry again, your sword of
flame, that you once placed in the hand of
the cherubim, 'to guard the way to the tree of
life.'* Now it is held in your own hand, also *Gen 3:24*
'guarding a way', the way to your holy thigh,
which is now a tree of life for all who take
hold of it. Until now it was indeed the cherubim who used this sword, the two-edged
sword of your burning love, so as to set themselves to a more stringent guarding of the
way of life, which the apostate angel and his
collaborator, sinful man, had kept so faithlessly, and thereby lost. Made all the more
eager by this negligence, the cherubim have
stood motionless upon their guard ever since.
From that day on, the flaming sword has
never fallen from their grasp. Because of it,
their hearts are continually inflamed with the
love of God, since, by a grace beyond price, it
has 'distinguished their cause from a nation
that is not holy.'* *Ps 43:1*

Yet, as we said, this sword was in their
hands, and they put it to very effectual use
upon themselves, but until the time of the
Lord's passion, it was very rarely brought
forth by the angels so as to pierce through the
hearts of men. So it is you, O mighty one,
who must gird it on; it is not without reason
that you carry a sword. You must draw it
once and for ever from its scabbard, 'to execute vengeance on the nations, and chastisement on the peoples,'* to set hearts on fire, *Ps 149:7*

to wound souls. That sword of yours is in every sense a sword of fire, flaming, glittering like lightning, beginning 'from the sanctuary of God',* from the holy of holies of your own self, Lord God. For you have not hesitated to use it on your self also, piercing your own self through; because of the very great love with which you loved us,* you surrendered your soul to death.* Yes, a mighty sword, and held in a mighty hand, that does not spare the only Son of God, 'reaching to the very division of the soul and spirit' in him.* It lays open to the whole world the divine tenderness of his heart, and pours it forth over all the earth.

Cf. Ez 9:6

Cf. Eph 2:4
Cf. Is 53:12

Heb 4:12

7. After this, will it seem strange to anyone if the sword of the Son of God, 'having drunk its fill in the heavens'* of his own blood, should pierce through your soul also, O holy mother of Jesus?* And so, coming down from those heavenly regions, it makes its way to right and left, wherever its edge is directed,* and nowhere does it spare or compassionate. For, seeing the great power of this sword and the great victory of the Son of God, who would not freely run forward to be wounded, making a willing and zealous offering of his soul to receive the wound of a love so great? In my case, I beseech you, do not hold back, O Lord my God, do not pass me over, do not treat me mildly! But 'let my soul die the death of the just',* the death of those you love and who love you.

Cf. Is 34:5

Cf. Lk 2:34

Cf. Ez 21:16

Num 23:10

Therefore, Lord, that sword of yours hangs above your thigh to guard it. Nobody, unless first pierced by that sword, and then set on fire and burnt to ashes, can approach the fountain of your most pure delight. Hidden within it is that most secret bone, which the Father fashioned in secret.* He wanted no one else to have any share in it, not one of the wise or learned to have any knowledge of it. That bone is exceedingly strong, rich tissue without and rich marrow within. In short, it was on this thigh bone of his Son that the Father set the distinctive seal of kinship and wrote a fresh inscription: 'King of kings and Lord of lords.'* For all who take their origin from that thigh, who drain the draught of that pleasure, are kings, sons of this king, heirs of this lordly one.

Cf. Ps 139:14

Rev 19:16

But who can describe the rare wonder of this begetting? Here your church, future mother of kings, is begotten from the thigh of your fruitful pleasure and pleasurable fruitfulness, while the sword of your charity wounds your heart. She is formed out of your bones and your flesh in the womb of your compassion, and she comes forth from your side, from a marriage bond and from a love that unites two in one. This begetting is without any doubt a rare and completely amazing marvel, all the more so in that it takes place, by and through your agency, when you yourself are dead. The very reason why this bride of yours is both living and the mother of all who live,* is that you laid down your life to make her live. So your daughter and your bride has the very greatest reasons for feeling a passionate and overwhelming love for you, her Father and her spouse. She would have the sword of your charity, which you have girded on your thigh, penetrate

Cf. Gen 3:20

from henceforth right up to the hilt, so that it pierces through her heart, because to beget and fashion her it first pierced your own soul, even unto death.

The bride is speaking here as one who is an intimate partner in the sacrament of Christ's death, and can explain its significance. The more deeply she loves it, the more fully she understands it, recalling it more frequently and pondering over it with greater happiness. In other words, she too bears upon her thigh the same sort of sword. By day and night she walks around the bed of her Solomon,* that is, her soul, her very body all helpless with love for him, so that, in her, as in his own bed, he may graciously choose to share her repose, and that it may be fitting for him to do so. She ponders continually on the reason that brought her into being and the ground from which she was fashioned, namely, God's love, so powerful, so deep a pleasure, producing so great a fruit. She lifts her eyes to that dwelling place in heaven, not made with human hands,* which is often, or, more truly, always the place where her thoughts dwell.* She blesses it, and all who live in it, because it rests upon these columns.

8. 'His legs', she says, 'are alabaster columns, set in sockets of pure gold.'* It would not be easy to say which of these columns is more precious or more beautiful, which is more massive or more lofty in height. For it was the Wisdom of God, wisest of architects, who 'built that house for himself.'* He measured out those columns with such delicate skill and judicial balance, and he designed

Cf. Sg 3:7

2 Cor 5:1

Ph 3:20

Sg 5:15

Pr 9:1

them for himself, so that the perpendicular of their equal height is not one least fraction of a degree out of true. They are made to harmonize with each other, to correspond together; and for all ages to come, holiness will be fruitful and sacred pleasure will be rich and full. Indeed, 'blessed are those who dwell in your house,'* Lord Jesus. You have made its columns so strong that your house need never dread a future day of destruction, as happened in the beginning. For in the beginning, your house was not built upon these columns, and so, when a great whirlwind came from north and struck its four corners, it left it a heap of ruins.* This is why it was in the hand of Solomon the wise, that is you, O Lord, that God the Father placed the work of rebuilding, giving you the role of architect. He wanted the house to rise up again from you, built on stronger columns and more solid foundations. And so, as we read in scripture, 'The latter splendor of this house shall be greater than the former, says the Lord of hosts.'*

Ps 84:4

Cf. Mt 7:27

Hag 2:10

Hence you came down from heaven, O Lord, my true Solomon, son of David, and you gave your whole heart to the task of building that was laid upon you. You swore a vow to the God of Jacob, that you would not lay your head on your pillow nor go to the bed of your repose, namely, the bosom of the Father, where you were before, until you found 'a place for the Lord, a dwelling for the God of Jacob.'* And so, in the rich variety of your holiness and in the sweetness of your love, by which you loved your bride,

Cf. Ps 132:2-5

fashioning and making her lovely through the power and charity of your death, you carved out from your own self and in your own self, the columns of your house. To this very day you press powerfully on with this task, skillfully intent upon it, and for us too, there will be 'no rest for our head', and no utter peace and perfect joy in heaven, until the last stone that this work requires, is set in place.

For you as well, my Lord, it will be a holy festivity and a sabbath of rare delight,* when your house is completely finished and made beautiful and you rest from all your labor.* From that day on, to live in your house will be as blissful as it is safe, founded as it will be upon those blissful and immovable columns. Moreover, the columns themselves 'are set in sockets of pure gold',* the twofold sockets of your humility. Without a doubt, the rock-like foundation of this whole huge erection is that your majesty stooped down to us from heaven, coming down in our flesh, and that you emptied out your glory for us, when you went up onto the cross. The bride does well to call these sockets 'pure gold', because all their material substance is of charity, and loving eyes see them irradiating the light of divine charity into the serene Jerusalem and the daughter of Zion, here in our midst.

Upon these foundations, then, rests the whole fabric of that heavenly mansion, and this is why, for all eternity, it will never be in danger of any accident. Spouse and bride may sleep in it in safety, taking their full delight in each other, and from that house may there ring out everlastingly the praise of those who

Cf. Is 58:13

Cf. Gen 2:1-3

Sg 5:15

bless and glorify the Father of the spouse,
and the spouse, his Son, and the Holy Spirit,
   one God, blessed and to be blessed,
      for ever and ever.
      Amen.

SERMON THIRTY-FOUR

The beginning of the thirty-fourth sermon.
Of the appearance of Jesus, which the bride compares to the appearance of an angel; and of the angelic appearance itself, which is holiness and peace and joy in the Holy Spirit; and how this appearance is incorruptible.

Sg 5:15

'HIS APPEARANCE is like Lebanon, choice as the cedars.'*

Sg 5:15

The voyage of the bride is nearly done. Over the sea of her beloved's praises, narrow but very deep, she has been borne by his Spirit's favoring gale, and now, prepared to furl her sails, she rolls up all that can be said in one brief and ingenious saying, and proclaims: 'His appearance is like Lebanon, choice as the cedars.'* It is as if she were to say to the maidens: How much longer shall I go on winding round and round? I can never catch up with his praise, and you can never catch up with me! He is greater than any praise, too high for any mind to understand. Indeed, I long for nothing more than to celebrate him as he deserves, but I fail completely, and I do not see how I shall ever succeed. He eludes all my efforts, hiding away in his sheer sublimity, and it is to those who are with him in his heavenly kingdom that he offers himself for praise and glory.

2. In the highest heaven, then, is his glory,* supremely radiant and sublime. There love burns bright and understanding is vigorous, there goodwill is ever eager and memory wide-awake. There no anxiety distracts, no difficulty presses, no fear disturbs, no hope seduces, but everything works together to praise and take delight in the Son of God. There 'day utters speech to day',* and I long to utter it to you, maidens, but this is a matter too high for me, and beyond all your capacities. Yet on that day of triumph in the height of heaven, when everyone is both a 'son of day'* and a 'day', 'day' truly 'utters speech to day',* one day crying aloud to another, 'In the beginning was the Word'* and 'the Word was made flesh.'*

Cf. Lk 2:14

Ps 19:2

Cf. 1 Thess 5:5
Ps 19:2
Jn 1:1
Jn 1:14

There it will be possible to know the joy of contemplating the appearance of my beloved with my own eyes, and of openly pointing him out to sight. So it is there that his appearance is celebrated with the delight that is his due,* since everything converges on it, and the one, tender desire of every loving heart is to be made like him. In short, there the appearance of my beloved diffuses itself throughout that whole sphere of light, pouring itself abroad without restraint, and thus wrests every eye impetuously to itself while it powerfully transforms every face into the likeness of its own brilliance.

Ps 147:1

So it is there that 'his appearance is like Lebanon,'* because there is no doubt that, together with him, there is a heavenly plantation of holy souls forming a true 'Lebanon'. For the true Lebanon is closely planted with a

Sg 5:15

great, towering mass of cedars. My spouse, that is, the true Solomon, built his house from them, and we read of it, 'It is a great house that I desire to build.'* And it was from this Lebanon that he came to us, as we find in the prophets, 'God has come from Lebanon, the holy one from the dense and shady mountain.'* Yes, from there he came to men, making himself lower than the angels,† and it was to Lebanon that he also returned, and his dwelling place is in its midst.

My beloved lives on Lebanon, there he takes his rest at noon,* there he pastures his flock among the lilies.* There the most beautiful and blessed of women,* his bride, who is in heaven and who knows not a moment's pause in the blissful and satisfying enjoyment of her spouse, who has him at her good pleasure, there she has the right to say, 'My beloved is mine and I am his, who feeds among the lilies.'* Yet even she, while she sojourns in this earthly desert, and can at times, in her ecstasy, apply the words of this song to herself, even she can scarcely do for half an hour what there she never ceases to do every hour.* For there at last is eternal life, and the full flood of those living waters which, flowing from her spouse, came down to the remote reaches of our distant valleys. But there is the well where they spring in abundance, there the great flood waters of their torrent, for there the Lord makes his dwelling so as to be throned as king for all eternity.*

3. If, then, something of his appearance

Margin notes:
2 Chron 2:5
Hab 3:3, used in the Office for Good Friday.
†Cf. Ps 8:5
Cf. Sg 1:6
Cf. Sg 2:16
Cf. Lk 1:42
Sg 6:2
Cf. Rev 8:1
Cf. Ps 29:9

irradiates our hearts here below, it comes from the fullness of this Lebanon, for it is from that Zion which is above, and is our mother,* that 'the appearance of his beauty shines.'* Even if it now lies hidden from mortal eyes, for here indeed we are walking 'in darkness and in the country of death's shadow,'* yet when he comes once more from heaven, attended by blessed troops of angels, then all eyes will clearly see that 'from Zion is the appearance of his beauty,'* because God will come in full sight. In the past, when he lived here in this land of ours, far from that Zion, he had a look that the very angels found wonderful and lovely. Even then he was easily the most beautiful to be seen of all the sons of men,* even more beautiful, to be precise, than the angels, but then 'cloud and darkness were round about' his appearance.* And hence those who were overshadowed by the same cloud, were accustomed to say, 'We saw him, and he had no appearance or beauty.'* His exceeding humility, which is the greatest part of Jesus' appearance, caused scandal to the sickly eye of fleshly wisdom, and what should have cured it, brought on blindness.

 4. Yet, among those lovely and choice cedars of Lebanon, from the very moment of his conception the appearance of Jesus aroused praise and wonder, glory and exultation. For cloud and darkness in no way clouded the sight of angels. For the angels, the light of his godhead shone only the brighter from that ethereal and gleaming cloud, and from it the Father's voice

Cf. Gal 4:16
Ps 50:2

Is 9:2

Ps 50:2

Cf. Ps 45:3

Ps 97:2

Is 53:2

thundered out to them more loudly, 'This is my beloved Son, in whom I am well pleased.'* From that very day, they set up for themselves a ladder of great loftiness and strength, by which they could ascend and descend upon the Son of man,* at every hour passing up and down these roads of life, without a pause. Here where there are so many thousands of ascents and descents, where there are such constant meetings and passings, in a wonderful way they never block or restrict one another. With wonderful gentleness and immense reverence, each strives to be the first to pay honor to the other,* and with courteous greetings, not as it does in this life but as treading the path that is Life, they defer to one another in loving rivalry. In fact, this is what is meant by 'the appearance of Lebanon', for, as the apostle says, 'The kingdom of God is holiness and peace and joy in the Holy Spirit.'* This is the loftiness of the cedars of Lebanon, this is the straightness, this is the sweet fragrance.

Mt 3:17

Cf. Jn 1:51

Cf. Rom 12:10

Rom 14:17

5. This is without any doubt the sublime justice of the angels, to contemplate God sublimely and stretch out to him with all their strength. Then this is their peace, that they mutually take delight in the Lord with the most selfless love. In this peace, their noble evenness leaves nothing twisted or out of line with the evenness of uprightness, as it is written, 'With God are dominion and fear, and he makes peace in the sublime heights of heaven.'* Finally, joy in the Holy Spirit the fruit, as we said above, of justice and peace, is the fragrance of their same trees. This is a

Job 25:2

scent most delicious to God and to their own selves, and they never cease to breathe it out from their own very beginning.

So this appearance of Lebanon is all the more lovely and seemly because of the nobility of its origin. Never, even for a moment, has it dishonored the beauty of its holiness; never, even for a moment, has it tempered it. Never, from the beginning of its blessed state, has the pupil of its eye turned away from the face of the Father and his only Son, not for one least flicker of the eyelid. Never have the borders of mutual love impinged upon one another, for he who 'makes peace in their borders',* has drawn those borders vast and infinite in range.

Cf. Ps 147:14

Joy, too, in the Holy Spirit is believed to be a sweetness that belonged originally to them because in those blessed throats it gives birth for all eternity to songs of jubilation and praise.

6. With good reason, then, does the bride compare the appearance of her beloved to the appearance of Lebanon for the beauty of the beloved keeps unimpaired the freshness it had at its birth and therefore is all the more noble, for while the other is destined at some time to fade, his beauty from the moment of its first flowering came forth never to perish. This explains why the spouse himself is called an angel by his Father. 'He will come,' he says, 'to his temple, the Lord whom you seek, the angel of the covenant whom you desire.'*

Mal 3:1

For being born of a virgin, he showed himself an angel not only in his charity and obedience, but also in his heavenly and taintless birth. Consequently, when the bride could find nothing among the sons of men to use as an example in describing the appearance of her beloved, truly more lovely to look at than any human being, she sought her comparison elsewhere, and took for her image the beautiful appearance of Lebanon.

7. For Lebanon is truly the virgin country of everlasting love, of unfallen holiness, of purest delight.* It is well named 'Lebanon', which means 'whiteness', for in the great fall of so many of the angels, it happily preserved the whiteness of its holiness, not only without loss, but even with an increase of beauty. Indeed, from that day, Lebanon became all the whiter because of 'the voice of the Lord breaking the cedars'.* It was those many cedars which had raised themselves on high above themselves, whose whiteness was changed and whose appearance became blacker than charcoal. But the whiteness of Lebanon came forth from this dark cloud in all its white radiance, cleaving firmly and purely forevermore to the whiteness of that eternal light, which is Christ.*

For its appearance is renewed day by day by the continual contemplation of the appearance of Christ, or rather, it becomes progressively more white. It tirelessly longs to change into his appearance, to transform its own into his. The height from which the cedars fell has given terrible proof of how their own nature can change, and the cedars who chose to take their stand in heaven, live in a blissful integrity, each in turn cleaving purely and soberly to their unchangeable

Cf. Qo 24:21

Cf. Ps 29:5

Cf. Wis 7:26

beginning, the only Son of the Father. The force of constant love keeps each in turn looking with unwavering gaze at the living source of their light. Solely through the free gift of his goodness, he divides light from darkness, so that, while darkness falls and fails, they themselves may become and remain 'light in the Lord.'* *Eph 5:8*

Thus the cedars of Lebanon are raised up to their fullest extent, but they are not lifted up with pride. They have no hesitation in reaching themselves out, but they are careful not to over-reach themselves. They spread their branches out to one another but never intertwine, they grow closely together without over-crowding, they cast a shade over themselves, yet never get in one another's light.

8. True enough, there is shadow even in that country of eternal brightness, since it contains a mountain, shady and densely planted, but it is only in order to refresh their mutual love in the Lord and deepen the reverence they feel for each other in Christ. The mountain is 'shady', because the nearer it is to eternal light, the more certainly and profoundly it understands, as if under the symbol of shadows, the nature of its own state and the inherent changeableness of its substance. And it is 'densely planted', but the denseness comes from a united throng of happy people, not from a disordered mob of malcontents. This 'denseness' is the united companionship of blessed spirits, where love is all eager for the same thing, all active for the same good. To be densely planted, each one for the sake of all, and all for the sake of

each, is to know a most pure and sweet enjoyment.

9. So the bride does well to apply the appearance of this lovely Lebanon to the most beautiful appearance of her beloved, yet even in this praise she preserves her usual restraint, for the comparison falls far short of perfection. For her spouse is the very Wisdom of God, and it is said of him, 'in appearance he is lovelier than the sun, and compared to the light, he is found the brighter.'* Yet however incomparable the appearance of his beauty, altogether beyond any just comparison, it does not forbid a partial comparison where there is a certain likeness. In the hands of the prophets, it graciously allows itself to be likened to many and various things, at their good pleasure, so how much more in the hands of the bride? And she, in her turn, holds out to the daughters of Jerusalem a most lucent mirror, full of grace, in which they may contemplate the appearance of her beloved.

10. But even on this mirror, the eyes of mortals cannot look long, because it is too bright. Only in shadow and in mystery is it possible, with side-long and fleeting glances, 'until day breathes and the shadows flee.'* But of course, at the breath of that most joyous day, when the shadows of all mysteries have fled far away, there will be no need of the mirror of comparisons. His very appearance will show itself quite openly, in fulfillment of the spouse's own words: 'I shall not then speak to you in parables, but I shall openly tell you of the Father.'*

May it be our privilege also, to rejoice with his bride and in her, in the joy of that blessed 'telling', on the day when all men see the beauty of the appearance of the spouse of the church, our Lord Jesus Christ, who together with God the Father
and the Holy Spirit, lives
and reigns, God,
for ever and
ever.
Amen.

SERMON THIRTY-FIVE

The beginning of the thirty-fifth sermon. Of the threefold appearance of the Lord Jesus, that is, of that which comes from his glorious union with the Word of God, of that which comes from his sacred, virginal conception, and of that which comes from his union with his holy body, which is the church.

Sg 5:15

'HIS APPEARANCE is like Lebanon.'* The beauty of Jesus, which exceeds all that can be denied and is desirable beyond anything that can be thought, presents a threefold aspect to those wishing to admire and reflect on it. There is the ideal, classic loveliness of his appearance, there is also his comely fairness, and finally, there is his grace and dignity.

It was the first of these that so impressed David at the very beginning of his marriage song. He placed it at the forefront of his praises: 'You have an ideal loveliness, greater than all the sons of men.'* That appearance is truly the loveliest of all appearances, for in it the virgin's son had the privilege of being taken up by the beauty of God, the only Son of the Father, and he takes wonderful glory from and in it. In this appearance, my Lord Jesus has shown himself so ideal in his surpassing beauty, for all who have the favor of

Ps 45:3

being admitted to his sight, that from then on, those who have seen this appearance once, yearn with insatiable desire for this appearance again, and for this appearance alone. Indeed, as it says of him in scripture, 'he is more beautiful than the sun,' wonderful 'above all the starry constellations.'* Wondering at him, every sense fails; longing for him, all seeing faints away; in comparison with him, all loveliness seems dim.

Wis 7:29

2. We can understand why the 'angels long to look upon'* this appearance, why they marvel to see him advancing towards them in the long robe of this incomparable loveliness, and why they cry: 'Who is this king of glory, this beautiful one in his long garment?'* This cry of admiration from the hearts and lips of the angels, has never ceased from the hour when the King of glory was clad by his Father in a robe of glory, crowned with the crown of the kingdom within his mother's womb. From then on, the stars of morning began to praise him, and all the sons of God to shout for joy.* The stars of morning were watching very eagerly for the morning rise of the eternal sun. They began to keep night watches of longing, in zealous anticipation of the first signs of his coming. They began to honor him with angelic praises, as he came, lifted up with the glory that is his due, hailing him as God, bowing low in adoration. I repeat, from that day on, there has always been 'glory in the heights of heaven',* in honor of the rising king. Jubilation has never faded from the heart nor praise from the lips nor contemplation from the

1 Pet 1:12

Ps 24:8, Is 63:1

Cf. Job 38:7

Cf. Lk 2:14

eye nor, in short, an insatiable longing from the soul. Furthermore, does not the Father of Lights himself also take pleasure in gazing on this appearance of Jesus? From that hour when he rested from all the works that he had done,* he gave himself completely to contemplating his appearance, taking his delight in that alone, with infinite pleasure.

Cf. Gen 2:3

3. A blessed day for you, Lord, which gladdened you with the glad announcement of your Son! Your Son, 'descended from David according to the flesh,'* your exceedingly beautiful Son, the perfect image of yourself, to the point that whoever sees him, will also see you!* On this day, and from this day on, may the day of my birth, as well as the night of my conception,* pass into oblivion forevermore. For this was why your Son was born, and why he came into the world,* that the appearance of his classic beauty, and the classic beauty of his appearance, might wipe away the disfigurement from the whole of his race. For this purpose, O loving Lord, in the wonderful working of your power, a Son was born to you and through your mercy, also for our sake, so that the very sight of his appearance might bring us back to you in friendship and incline you to us in love.

Rom 1:3

Cf. Jn 14:9

Cf. Job 3:3

Cf. Jn 3:19

4. O holy Father, how we thank you! From that day you have taken such delight in this appearance of your Son, that for his sake you have determined to show mercy to all his race. You have forgotten all your just anger,* so that you do not only delight in him yourself, but in him and with him, we too, begin

Cf. Ps 85:3

Sermon Thirty-Five

to be a delight to you. In a word, it has been your good pleasure that we also should become and be called your sons,* in your Son, and with him. Still, as is only fitting, the Son who was born to you from the virgin daughter of David,* is your Son in a much more splendid way and with nobler dignity. He is Son by reason of the grace of that most holy union which unites him in oneness of person to your only-begotten Son. But as for us, we are sons through grace of adoption, and it was through him that you adopted us and united us to him in faith and love.

Cf. 1 Jn 3:1

Cf. Is 9:6

O Father, it was your love that made you send forth the splendor of your glory to become intimately united with this man, the virgin's son, and it was love that made you clothe him with the robe of ideal beauty, to the glory and honor of all his brothers, your sons. Truly, Lord, it is this love of yours, this tender courtesy, this grace that makes your new creation radiantly white. This is 'the mountain of your holiness',* the mountain on which you planted your great cedars which are always with you.* It was surely on this mountain that all the choice cedars put down deep roots from the beginning, when the voice of your thunder shattered and overwhelmed those Lebanon cedars that had reached out above themselves, glorying not in you, but in themselves, in your despite.* So from that day on, those cedars that were left, the ones who were saved,* stood unshaken and unwithering on the mountain of Lebanon, of 'their whiteness', which is your

Cf. Ps 78:55

Cf. Mt 18:10

Cf. Rom 11:5

Cf. Rom 9:27

own self. In a wonderful way, what had before been liable to decay, was now clad in incorruption because of the corruption of the other cedars, and it was in the blood of the wicked that the blessed were made white. For, cleaving with the whole strength of their roots to you, the purest and truest whiteness, they have, for ever after, in their very origin and foundation, a perennial and continual whiteness making them radiantly white.

In your own wonderful fashion, you glorified the appearance of our Lord, the virgin's son, giving him 'that name which is above all names',* so that he might truly be and truly be called, your Sole-begotten One. That lovely appearance of his, like the appearance of Lebanon, makes firm and holds together all the cedars you have planted, irradiating and renewing them in the whiteness of the eternal light, which is himself.* In fact, he is himself the mountain you have consecrated for your own, the 'mountain where you have been pleased to make your dwelling,'* the mountain facing south, upon which you build your dwelling place and the temple of your glory.* And then, from the foot of this mountain of Lebanon, on which you have set your heavenly Jerusalem, your compassion made a Jordan spring up for us, through the coming to our world of your Son. It sent down rich streams of living waters from on high, washing us clean, whether by the mystery of baptism or sacramental penance.*

Lord, it was one and the same love that stretched out to both angel and man, preserving one and saving the other. This, then, is that wonderful and truly glorious appearance of the Lord Jesus, on which, Lord, your eyes are always resting. His appearance is like Lebanon, because in every respect it is like the appearance of your own beauty. This is why this appearance gives you such intense delight, being 'the radiant mirror of your majesty and the image of your goodness,'* showing you within itself a most faithful picture of what you are, a most perfect representation. *Wis 7:26*

This is the sheer, classic loveliness of the appearance of the Lord Jesus.

5. Next, there is the beauty of his appearance with respect to the special graces that are his in his humanity. In these purely human qualities, also, he shows himself as lovelier than all the sons of men,* and in this appearance too, he shines with wonderful brightness before the eyes of his lovers. For here too, he is very fair, 'above all the starry constellations,'* as scripture says, because all the virtues of the saints draw their brightness from his virtue, shining forth with incomparable splendor. If we ponder on each of the virtues of this man, one by one: his innocence, his gentleness, his humility, his patience, his kindness, justice, compassion, love—the beauty of his appearance is infinite, and there is nothing in all the glories of the saints that can fitly be held up in comparison. *Cf. Ps 45:3* *Wis 7:29*

Beloved brothers, for me, this appearance of my Lord is like an intimate looking glass, and I trust in the Lord Jesus that this is so for you, also, whenever you want to look hard at the stains on your face, without any pretence or human respect. Indeed, in his innocence, I blush to see my own impurity; in his gentleness, I am ashamed of my own harsh dealings; his humility gives me a loathing for my own pride; in his patience I look upon my own impatience with confusion; in his goodness, I suffer the pain of seeing my own evil; in his justice, the full malice of my injustice comes home to me; in his compassion, I see how wrong is my lack of compassion; in his love, whether for God or for neighbor, I understand fully how I fail in both, and I grieve over it.

The appearance of which I spoke of a little while before, I described as being the mirror of God's majesty, always in God's hand,* and so not in keeping with my poverty, nor accessible to it. But to confront my face in this human mirror, as far as I am able by his merciful favor, is a task burdensome but not fruitless. As I have clearly proved by experience indeed, you have proved it too, I know and believe there is nothing more profitable, nothing more efficacious able to be imagined, if we want to change our ugliness into beauty, or increase what beauty there is, and conform it more fully to your beauty.

Just consider whether all the words of the psalms which I quote above, do not come down basically to this meaning: 'In your lovely appearance and your beauty, turn, go forth triumphantly, and reign.'* It says: 'In your lovely appearance and your beauty, turn,' as if to imply: Show your appearance and your beauty, and make those

Sermon Thirty-Five

who love you turn this gaze on that beauty. If they gaze earnestly on it, you will go forth triumphantly; for if they gaze on your appearance and beauty, then you can establish in them the kingdom of your glory. For to gaze earnestly and devotedly on the appearance and beauty of Jesus is truly a triumphant and speedy progress to his kingdom. Continually to gaze on it is to be constantly renewed in spirit and, in a sense, to be perpetually made a shining white. So of this appearance, also, the bride has every reason to say: 'His appearance is like Lebanon.'* *Sg 5:15* Clearly, we never gaze on that appearance in vain. We never contemplate it without some traces of our ugliness being removed, some treasures of beauty being acquired. Approach it frequently, brothers; this is the advice of the Holy Spirit. Come close, and in the light of the appearance of Jesus, be filled with light, be radiantly white and be made new.* *Cf. Ps 34:6*

6. I understand yet a further meaning underlying these words, one I touched upon in the preceding sermon. Lebanon may be taken as the sacred and uniquely wonderful occurrence of the birth of Christ according to the flesh. That, then, is the whiteness of our birth, having his appearance and beauty, the grace of a twofold whiteness. For his spotless flesh, from the virgin's womb, like a stone hewn from the mountain without human hands,* clothed that new man with a *Cf. Dan 2:34* new appearance. And then the soul of Jesus, itself, filled with grace and truth,* brought *Cf. Jn 1:14* the honor of a fresh beauty to the flesh received from the virgin. So this appearance

of Jesus is like Lebanon, pure from its beginning, as if it were some perenniel spring of whiteness. It protected Jesus himself from the very least stain of sin, and is a continual source of whiteness for the washing away of our shames.

As I mentioned before, the third aspect of Jesus, beauty, can be seen clearly in those things that are connected with him. I have dealt with the glory of his appearance of inexpressible, classic loveliness, as Son of God. I have also dealt with his appearance of infinitely comely fairness, as son of the virgin, overflowing vessel of all the virtues. But all this appearance of beauty would be for himself alone, if he did not have a bride for whom such beauty was seemly, and whose appearance would be beautiful because of his. After all, the apostle tells us that 'a man's glory is his wife.'* If the Father alone took pleasure in the appearance of his Son, and there was glory only to God in the heights of heaven,* my Lord Jesus would certainly have an ideal beauty and a comely fairness, but perhaps there would be less grace and dignity. But as it is, when the Father gave him this lovely bride in the union of marriage, he bestowed on him 'glory and great dignity'.*

7. The first two aspects of his beauty which I spoke of above, are so great that they cannot be increased. But the appearance of his grace and dignity grows daily by continual and very abundant increase. Moreover, when David broke forth into the 'goodly theme of his marriage song',* he did not overlook this appearance in his hymn of praise. This is

1 Cor 11:7

Cf. Lk 2:14

Ps 21:6

Cf. Ps 45:1

why, having joyously and sweetly sung the exquisite glory of the spouse, he did not then leave him there in solitary loveliness, without a bride. The song of praise continued: 'The queen stands at your right in golden attire.'* *Ps 45:9* Indeed, a solitary glory comes short of the fulness of glory, and it does not rise to the heights of appreciation until it is without the stern shadow of solitude or the reproach of bereavement. Obviously, however great the glory, it loses something if there is no one to see it as glory. If there is no fellowship leading naturally to a common sharing, then glory will have no glory, for it all remains deep within itself. So we see from the very beginning of creation how the Father made provision in advance for his Son to appear in his full beauty. 'It is not good,' he said, 'for man to be alone.'* *Gen 2:18* It was for this reason that the Father made for his Son 'a helper fit for him.'* *Gen 2:18* He fashioned from his side a woman *Cf. Gen 1:26* who was his perfect 'image and likeness',* one who could 'sleep in his bosom and warm the Lord her king.'* *1 Kings 1:2* How 'can a man sleep alone and be warm?' But, 'if there are two sleeping together, they give warmth to each other,'* equally. *Eccles 4:11*

So then to have nothing lacking to his Son's dignity, God pressed on, day by day adding to the 'life of the king'* from the *Cf. Ps 61:6* dignity of his bride. He labors over this right up to the present time, or rather, this will be his labor until the end of time, until he has brought to its full the great grace and dignity he intends for his Son. Indeed, until that is completed, there will be no sabbath in heaven, and no time for rest on earth. But when God has brought his work to completion, then there will come forth 'the spouse from his room and the bride from her chamber,'* so that 'out of Sion, the appearance of his grace and dignity',* now at the full of its perfection, may shine out to all the blessed, when God will come in the company of that beauty to show himself our judge. Then the queen, who till that day has stood at his side, working with her spouse and pleading for the salvation of her children, will there and then have the bliss of hearing from him: 'Sit at my right side.'* From that hour, she will be sitting at the side of her spouse, sleeping at the side of him from whom she was taken. 'They will be two in one flesh,'* yes, and in one voice, also. For the spouse, speaking in the voice of spouse and bride, will rejoice in that day, crying aloud: 'How joyfully I delight in the Lord, my spirit leaping up to my God! He has clothed me with the garments of salvation, he has covered me with the robe of righteousness, as a bridegroom adorned with a garland, as a bride arrayed in her jewels.'*

On that day, we shall see with our own eyes how truly the bride spoke of her spouse: 'His appearance is like Lebanon.'* On that day, the dignity of Jesus' appearance will be perfectly fulfilled in the dignity of his bride, giving her, too, the right to be called 'Lebanon'. Made spotlessly white by her white spouse, all her cedars given back to her, she has nothing more to stretch out for on longing, nothing to fear. On that day, may we too be remembered as part of the beauty of

his bride, by the Son of God, most beautiful in appearance, who with his Father and the Holy Spirit, lives and reigns,
God, for ever and ever.
Amen.

SERMON THIRTY-SIX

The beginning of the thirty-sixth sermon. Of the humility of Jesus, and the pride of Lucifer.

Sg 5:15

Cf. 1 Cor 1:25
1 Cor 2:6

'CHOICE AS THE CEDARS.'* I put it to you, what is the meaning of faint and meager praise, especially if this is the note on which we are to end? In the marketplace, merchants anxious to make a deal, keep the firm and high-sounding phrases of their eulogies for the very end of the description in the hope that their hearers may receive the most powerful impression at the finish, and, emotionally stirred, immediately make up their mind. But the bride is not versed in the wisdom of this world, rather because she is bride to the Word of God, and her foolishness is wiser than men.* It is among 'the perfect' that she 'speaks wisdom',* and to this kind of wise man that she teaches at greater depth. She has woven a cloak of praise for her beloved, and she wants it finished off with golden fringes. So, after the long rollcall of his praises, she adds at the last praise of his humility.

The bride has made a wise decision. All the virtues, not only of men of virtue, but even of the very Lord of virtues, find their completion in humility. This is why her spouse is wonderful both in heaven and on earth. He is the First, and 'his glory is above the heavens,'* and yet at the same time, he is the last, and his humility is lower than the very lowest of the lowly. So the bride, well aware of this mystery, for she has learned, in the Spirit of God, to search all things, even the depths of the Spirit,* add to her loving description of his beauty by praise of his humility, which is the highest praise his beauty can have.

Ps 113:4

Cf. 1 Cor 2:10

Therefore the bride says: 'His appearance is like that of Lebanon, choice as one of its cedars.'* It is as if she were to say: Although the marvelous power of his beauty makes him incomparably more glorious than all God's chosen ones, nevertheless, in his humility, he makes himself like the others, counting himself among the cedars of God. He forgets the honor that is his due, and devotes himself wholly to loveliness. It costs him nothing to break up, as it were, the glory of his appearance and bequeath it to his little ones to be their glory. He lays aside his primacy, and hands himself over even to the least of his members in a state of complete sharing and equality. 'God, above all things and blessed for ever',* makes it his glory to become like a cedar planted on Lebanon, standing among the other cedars and stretching out to them his branches.*

Sg 5:15

Rom 9:5

Cf. Qo 50:13

So, in the eyes of those who love the appearance of Jesus, and gaze on it directly, his beauty is all the more wonderful for his placing himself at the feet of all in humility, as though he no longer remembered that he was wonderful or lovely in appearance.

2. The bride does well, then, very well and laudably, to speak with eloquence of the tassels fringing her spouse's robe. She has certain knowledge of their strength and beauty. It is my belief that she has learned by experience that in them is to be found great relief and healing for a swelling sore and a gaping wound. She knows, too, how quickly, when she has despaired of all other doctors and medicines, her flow of blood has been staunched by merely touching them.* There- *Cf. Mt 9:20* fore, as far as the bride is concerned, these commendations of the tassels of his robe are wholly without trace of 'the leaven of the pharisees.'* In her hands, we find genuine *Mk 8:15* praise of Christ's genuine humility; there is certainly nothing feigned. In short, with all her strength she pursues her end unswervingly, namely, to please him whose approval she covets, and for the king to desire her beauty.* *Cf. Ps 45:12* So with ease and joy she often watches herself reflected in the mirror of Christ's humility, as if she heard her spouse saying to her, 'Go, and do likewise.'* *Lk 10:37*

3. The cedar whose heart was lifted up by its own greatness, and who had lost, as scripture says, wisdom because of its beauty,* did *Cf. Ez 28:17* not know the power of this mystery. It possessed indeed very great wisdom, and even to this day, not, though for its own good it has kept the shadowy form of it. But it used wisdom wrongly, to its own destruction and, as far as it possibly could, the destruction of all creation. From being the wisest, it became the most cunning of creatures. So we read: 'The serpent was the most

cunning of all the living things the Lord God had made.'* Surely there was an amazingly fine imitation of wisdom for it to be written, 'See, you are wiser than Daniel, and no mystery is hidden from you'?* And was it not a cedar of very great loftiness of which it could be said: 'No cedar in God's paradise was of more towering height than that cedar', all the ornamental trees and cedars envied it, and 'the fir trees could not come up to its boughs'?* This is not surprising. As the prophet says, 'The waters nourished it, the deep made it grow tall,'* meaning, the waters of immense knowledge, and the deep of infinite wisdom. Indeed, as scripture has it, it made those waters flow 'to all the trees' of the heavenly country in which it is planted, and 'therefore, it towered high above them all.'*

Gen 3:1

Ez 28:3

Ez 31:8

Ez 31:4

Ez 31:4

So then, that cedar possessed height from searching into the mysteries of God, it possessed strength from recognizing the power of God, it possessed uprightness from contemplating the justice of God, it possessed a sweet scent from thinking of the goodness of God, it possessed a fadeless youth from understanding the eternity of God and from its own everlasting and immortal substance, and, finally, it possessed wide-spreading branches, from its magnificent and superabundant knowledge. At the same time, from all these qualities, it possessed an incomparable beauty, and, on the word of scripture, all the other trees marvelled at it and tried to rival it.* Surely the bride's words of praise, 'His appearance is like Lebanon' would seem to fit this cedar very well?*

Cf. Ez 31:9

Sg 5:15

4. Yet what comes next does not fit so smoothly: 'Chosen as one of the cedars.'* Lifted up above the cedars, yes, but not 'chosen as one of the cedars'. In fact, the prophet tells that Lebanon opened its gates, and fire devoured its cedars.* In all he did this begetter of arrogance and ingratitude gave no honor to the God who had created him more noble than any other creature. He boasted rather of what he had received as though it were his own doing,* he claimed God's gift as his very own, and like a thief, he took as his rightful due the glory that belongs to God. In his eager pursuit of self-aggrandisement, 'his heart', as scripture says, 'became filled with turmoil,'* and what he had so freely conceived in and of himself, he brought forth and passed over to his brethren. He gloried in his greater excellence, he aspired to be their overlord, to the extent of setting his throne on high, above the stars of God.* He gloried, in fact, not so much in his greatness, as in being greater than others, uniquely great.

Hence the spirit of pride, which he had brought forth from his own heart, led him to plunder with ruthless arrogance what belonged to the common good. He took for his own private and particular use what had been created for the use of all, namely, the beauty he had been given. Indeed, breathing out nothing but ambition, he labored to take into his own control not only the good within himself, but even the glory of all his fellows. Yet what compassion one feels for the poor wretches who, as scripture says, foolishly took hold of the shadow which he held out to them. They built

Sg 5:15

Cf. Zech 11:1

Cf. 1 Cor 4:7

Ez 28:16

Cf. Is 14:13

Sermon Thirty-Six

their nests in his leaves, and when the time came for his branches to be shattered, they too fell violently to earth in his fall.* *Cf. Ez 31:6, 12*

But the ambition of this proud and restless cedar did not stop here. As we find said of him, 'he enlarged his spirit, and opened his mouth beyond measure,'* and he set his *Is 5:14* sights on coveting the inexpressible glory of the Son of God. With still greater effrontery, this blasphemer even had the temerity to count on the glory to which he aspired, to the point of saying 'in his foolish heart: I shall be like the Most High.'* First, then, he *Ps 14:1 &* brought destruction on his own head, next he *Is 14:14* was responsible for the loss of all his brethren, and finally, laying arrogant and greedy hands on the very majesty of God, he set all heaven in a turmoil with his ambition. And when the powers of heaven could endure it no longer, they contemptuously cast out the sacrilegious thief, brigand and traitor, and strife went out with him.* *Cf. Pr 22:10*

5. Yet it was not only he who went out. He plucked up by the roots a great number of cedars who had imitated his pride and agreed with his ambition, and he transplanted them to this world of mist. But here they could not remain for long. There is no place fit for such great ambition except the lake of the deepest abasement. Yet not even here, in that prison in which the damned are thrust, 'while a pit is dug for the wicked,'* no, not even here, is *Ps 94:13* ambition still or pride at rest. In every way possible, it tries to prevent the rebuilding of the ruins of Lebanon, for which it was responsible. When it was in heaven, it possessed

the glory of being like God, and now, on earth, it hastily snatches at it and takes it for its own, by inventing idolatry, with unheard of folly and shamelessness.

Although he saw the fires of avenging flame which had been prepared for him from the beginning,* yet all this only made him hard as stone, scorning the deep as a thing outworn.* For nothing that he saw did he become less fierce; on the contrary, he grew harsher, like an anvil under the hammerer.* So with full understanding and vision, he goes on kindling a fire for himself, where he is destined to burn to ash for all eternity. He brings to that fire as much wood as he can, carrying it on his own shoulders and on those of all his servants. Surely it is in the just designs of God that he digs a pit for himself, that he lays a snare for himself, that he sets an ambush for himself,* that he kindles, as I have said, his own fire. He could have found no one better fitted for this purpose, no one more cunning or bold or cruel or skilful.

This gives a special relevance to what the Lord says of him: 'See, I have created a smith who blows the coals of the fire and produces a vessel for his work; and I have also created the murderer to destroy.'* He heaps up the coals with wonderful and eager zeal, and when they are heaped, he never stops blowing on them so as to forge his own destruction. He makes it his purpose to stain more deeply still in dirt that beauty of Lebanon which once shone in him, but now has lost its brightness, until that brightness loses all its color and becomes most ugly;* and thus that glorious beauty, so rashly sought may be vindicated and reclaimed for the Only-begotten of the Father.

6. When 'all the ends of the earth see the salvation of our God,'* and see, on the one hand, Christ in all the glory of his ineffable loveliness, and on the other, anything but glorious, the evil one in the foul cloud of his hideousness, then in this comparison, his face will reflect the arrogance that belongs to him and all the sons of pride,* while the face of Christ Jesus will testify to his humility and that of all who share his wisdom. Hence it will be said by those who look at him on that day, and laugh: 'There he is, the disturber, who hankered after the position of God's Son; there he is, the one who unsettled heaven and earth, who damned creation, who murdered the Creator; look, there is the one who wanted to be first, now taking his place as the last and least. So all creation will rightly rise against him. Shattered by the thunder of God's majesty, struck by his lightning, burnt to ashes, he will fall headlong in the sight of all.

Then in comparison with his terrible repulsiveness, the appearance of Jesus will be even more beautiful than before, and it will be said to him: 'Truly, Lord our God, you are beautiful and gracious, and in either of your natures the classic grace of your loveliness is very wonderful. Although in your divine essence you are truly coequal with your Father, you have come down to the depths of human nature in order to restore what the rival of your glory violated. He set his heart

Is 52:10

Cf. Hos 5:5

on the highest place, you submitted to the lowest. His ambition was to lord it over the heavens, yours to be a servant on the earth, and, what is humbler still, to be the servant of sinners. 'He, the beginning of all the ways of God,'* was the beginning and cause of ruin; you, the first beginning of all that is, are the beginning and cause of restoration. He was set in the heavens, highest of the angels and nearest to God, and he fouled his beauty and tainted the glory of his fellows; you were clothed in flesh, born of a woman, living among sinners, and you kept yourself free from stain and bore the sin of the world.*

Yet nonetheless, your humanity, too, has infinite beauty. Although in that humanity you were taken up by the very form of God, you did not relish your greatness, but conformed yourself to our nature and made yourself like the humble. In consequence, you have the glorious position that Lucifer desired, you made 'like the Most High',* indeed, you are the Son of the most High: yet this high dignity did not raise your heart to pride. From the hour of your conception, when you were adopted by the Son of God, you never cease giving thanks to the Lord God your protector. Your heart is full of prayer and thanksgiving to the God of your life, and you cry out to God, 'You are my Protector'.*

That is why, though your appearance may be 'as Lebanon', you are nevertheless 'choice as the cedars',* most humbly obedient to the election by which God chose to take you up, and abasing yourself before the majesty

Sermon Thirty-Six

through which and in which you were exalted, giving incomparable thanks for the grace by which grace and glory were lavished upon you. In short, although, O Lord our God, you are great beyond all measure,* you came to live among your little ones as one of them.* You did more. Taking up the burden of every kind of service, you emptied yourself completely and put yourself at their feet, not their fellow-servant, but their drudge.* Even on your throne at the right hand of your Father, you have not laid aside, for one moment, the measure of your earlier humility, so that to all ages, you are both the highest of all and, equally, the lowest. May you hold in everything the primacy,* as is only right, for you live and reign, with God the Father
and the Holy Spirit, God,
for ever and ever.
Amen.

Cf. Ps 104:1
Cf. Qo 32:1

Cf. Guerric, Sermon I.1 for Palm Sunday; PL 185:1280; CF 32:55-6.

Cf. Col 1:18

SERMON THIRTY-SEVEN

The beginning of the thirty-seventh sermon.
Of the throat of the spouse, which enables him to distinguish the tastes of various foods, and what his foods are.

Sg 5:16

'HIS THROAT is most sweet, and he is wholly desirable.'*
In the rollcall of her beloved's praises, it would seem that his throat, which the bride describes as 'most sweet', should come before his hands or his belly or his legs. Yet this is purposely kept to the very end, and it seems to me for a special reason, namely, that the whole eulogy may be seasoned by this sweetness. For it is worth noting that in these words of praise, the bride has no recourse to images of comparison, as in all the other loving expressions she employs in her beloved's praise. For example, she calls his head 'purest gold',* she describes his locks as 'lofty palm trees',* and in this way she finds an apt comparison for everything else she speaks of. But when she comes to eulogize his throat, she discards the veil of imagery, and simply says, 'most sweet'. Then she rounds off her hymn of praise with the words: 'He is wholly desirable'.*

Sg 5:11
Sg 5:11

Sg 5:16

2. Unless you have a better suggestion, I take it that the bride means the 'throat' of

the spouse to signify the pleasant sweetness of the interior 'tasting' with which the spouse distinguishes the different foods that sustain his human life, as well as the different tastes of these foods. For not everything tastes alike. One food differs from another, not only in its nature but also in its sweetness. Butter has one flavor, and honey another; honey in its pure state differs again from honey in the comb, as bread does from fish, and milk from wine, and fresh fruit from dried. It was the first two, namely, butter and honey, that Isaiah prophesied Christ was to eat, either in childhood or from his childhood on.* Scripture tells us that after his resurrection, he was offered a comb of honey,* and he himself, speaking to his bride, makes it clear that he ate the comb with its honey.* Without doubt, he also ate bread both before and after his resurrection, while the gospel makes mention too, that he partook of fish after he had risen.* Then again, his own words to the bride are proof of his drinking wine with milk.* Lastly, his bride refers to both fresh and dried fruit; 'For you, my beloved, I have laid up fruit, fresh as well as dried.'* Obviously the intention is for him to be refreshed with their scent and flavor, at his choice.

 Who is able to grasp the varied flavors of all these, and how one flavor differs from another? And even if one were to grasp something of it all, what hope is there of conveying their true figurative meaning? Yet we do not want to ignore completely these things that have encountered us in passing, so I shall see to it that you at least have the opportunity

Cf. Is 7:15

Cf. Lk 24:42

Cf. Sg 5:1

Cf. Lk 24:42
Cf. Sg 5:1

Sg 7:13

to become 'the wise man who hears', when something is said, and 'becomes wiser'.* As scripture says, he grows in wisdom.*

So then, one might call butter a rich, smooth disposition of charity, sharing through love in all our brother's concerns, good and bad. This food belongs especially to the time of youth, coming as a richer food after the milk of childlike innocence. Not only does it bring the sweetness of simple innocence to throat and palate, but the richness of its kindness provides the throat with savor and enriches the mind. Moreover, to the making of this food there goes, not less milk, but a far greater amount, for, as Isaiah says, from the great abundance of milk, he will eat butter.*

3. Without too much incongruity, let me give the name of 'honey' to the sweetness of glory which true Christian hearts, eager for the glory that comes from God, gather for themselves from various flowers. And, not only from perfect flowers, of those that cannot fade, but, surprisingly, even from the flowers of the field, blooming today and tomorrow cast into the oven.* In fact, in this passing fleshly glory, which the Holy Spirit, through the lips of Isaiah, compares to the flower of the field,* it is possible, by holy meditation, to extract an imperishable glory, if only you are rich in those keen desires which made holy by the Holy Spirit have learnt the way of making this honey. Any flower at all, however insignificant, is still an unique mirror of God's eternal glory. It has this tremendous

importance, that in it we can see reflected something of the glory of the Lord. For that heavenly beauty, of which the psalm sings: 'All the beauty of the meadow is mine,'* seems to have left some traces of its beauty, however remote and unlike in glory, in this 'beauty of the meadow', which is here among men, that is, the glory of the world. Anyone who makes wise use of it, can gather from its flowers the sweetest of honeys. With that honey in his mouth, he will acquire the experience that makes the glory of the world appear like a nauseating bitterness, and that makes his throat eager for the glory which is in heaven, the pure honey of glory. This is why scripture, speaking of the qualities of honey mixed with butter, says that the use of these foods brings to a man the knowledge of how to reject evil and choose good.*

Ps 50:11

Cf. Is 7:15

4. This sweet and gentle training is well suited to the boyhood of our Emmanuel. It is not that he needs these flowers in order to contemplate the unseen glory of God, being himself nothing less than the flower of the meadow* from whom the whole swarm of heavenly bees gather the finest and rarest honey. But the Wisdom of God, taking flesh, wished to live like us, and in this way he chose to savor to the full whatever was human, and to change into the contemplation of heavenly things whatever he experienced in his fleshly senses.*

Cf. Sg 2:1

Cf. Rom 8:5

Yet, in another respect, fed every hour on the sweetness of the sacred honey that was within him, he was himself that honey. It was stored up for him in that honeycomb which the Wisdom of God so wonderfully fashioned, had wisely built for himself when he took his spotless body from the virgin.* His great glory is that honey, placed in the comb and there concealed, growing ever sweeter within the virginal body and marvelously containing itself within those virginal limits.

Cf. Jn 1:14

Whenever he chooses, then, our Emmanuel eats, now his pure honey, now the honeycomb with his honey. The virgin's son has equal freedom to glory at his good pleasure in the greatness of the Word who lifts him up, and to render indescribable and most glorious thanks to God the Father and to His Word, because in lifting up his flesh, the Word has given it such joy. But after the triumph of the resurrection he alone has the right to glory and to say to his bride, 'I eat my honeycomb with my honey,'* in other words, through the glory of his resurrection the honey has been returned to the wax from which it came. It is not that the Word deserted even for a moment the honeycomb of the flesh he once assumed; rather with the total extinction of mortality he has now totally steeped and clothed his flesh with the glory of a new immortality never henceforth to be shed for all eternity.*

Sg 5:1

Cf. 1 Cor 15:54

5. Do you too long to feed Jesus with food like this? Do you too want to prepare for his 'most sweet throat', the delicacies he loves? Then, in the secrecy of your heart, like the ingenious bee, first hang up the clinging wax of holy thoughts, breathing out the love of Christ. And thereafter drench them with

loving dispositions, as if sprinkling them with a honeyed dew. The Holy Spirit will help you to arrange your comb by the skilful dexterity of your hands and feet, so that one meditation harmoniously follows another, and, each helping the other with identical support and mutual aid, they can together raise a marvelous structure for the angels to gaze upon. Then you will be able to gather for yourself honey from 'the beauty of the meadow',* *Ps 50:11* which is not on this earth, from the roses and lilies of the valley, among which the beloved makes his pasture,* that is, from the holy joy *Cf. Sg 2:16* of the celestial spirits. Above all, you will be able to gather honey from that flower on which rests the sevenfold Spirit,* because in *Cf. Is 11:2* him dwells all the fulness of what is sweet.* *Cf. Col 1:19* The oftener you come to suck his honey, the more blooming you will find him, and the more overflowing. Eagerly, then, buzz round that flower, and lose yourself within its holy depths. He himself must first feed you on himself, and then in time to come, you in turn will be able to feed him.

Moreover, whatever the loving sweetness you draw from him in your love, do not lose it by betraying it, do not betray yourself by losing it! Carry that gift of heavenly bounty away into the secret chambers of your heart, digest it and conceal it. Imitate the wisdom of that most prudent of bees, of whom it is written: 'Mary kept all these words, storing them in her heart.'* Believe me, the Lord *Lk 2:19* Jesus will be more delightfully fed by a honeycomb of this kind of honey, than by honey that flows from your hand. As Solomon says, 'It is the glory of God to conceal his word'.* To a great extent, the very concealment of glory confers a certain degree of taste in the glory itself, and for this reason the throat knows very much more sweetness.

6. As for bread and fish, although I read that they were offered Jesus after his resurrection,* nobody can deny that he also ate them before his resurrection, but in a different manner. Before his resurrection he ate his bread in the sweat of his brow,* since the near approach of his passion made him say to his Father in anguish, 'Not what I will, but what you will.'* The very bread of Jesus, and also that of angels,* is to do the Father's will. But in the days of his flesh, when he was prone to suffering, that bread was, as it were, mingled with ashes of repentance.* Clearly its taste was not the same as the bread of his resurrection, gleaming white, pure bread of the finest wheaten flour.

The fish of patience, too, which are tossed this way and that by the waves of the sea, finding life where all other living things find death, came to the shore of the resurrection to be in contact with Jesus. For Jesus risen from the dead, stood on the shore;* and it tasted very different from the days of his passion, when suffering produced patience.* Indeed, there are within him infinite riches of patience, yet every fish of this kind has about it something of the grilled fish of his resurrection,* a certain marvelous flavor of impassibility and pure joy.

If you also want to refresh Jesus with these foods, you must come to the point of saying

with him: 'My food is to do the will of my Father who is in heaven.'* *Jn 4:34*
You must even say with the apostle, 'Gladly will I glory in my infirmities.'* *2 Cor 12:9*
You will show that you have risen with Christ and are 'walking in newness of life',* *Cf. Rom 6:4*
if you offer both these foods to Christ, while at the same time, sitting down to eat with him.

7. Before he suffered his passion, Jesus promised his disciples that after his resurrection he would 'drink new wine with them',* *Cf. Mt 26:29*
and who can doubt but that he kept his promise? But in speaking of 'new', he clearly implied a reference to the 'old wine', making a clear distinction between the happiness and glow of love that belong to our present pilgrimage through the valley of the shadow of death,* *Cf. Ps 23:4*
and that rich and fertile love which the vine bears in the kingdom of God, in the land of the living. And this is the wine that he says he has blended with milk, telling his bride, 'I drink my wine with my milk.'* *Sg 5:1*
We must not pass over his special mention of 'mine', by which he intended to signify the new wine, as that was more in keeping with him than the old.

Yet, because it is this new wine, namely, the ineffable joy of the newness of life that comes from his resurrection, which he drinks with his disciples, they like little children are as yet not strong enough to bear the newness of this great joy. Therefore the Wisdom of God mixes with his wine* *Cf. Pr 9:2*
a little milk of the kind of joy they can understand. According to what he sees to be their capacity, he offers it first in the appearance of a stranger, and

then in one they know well, subduing the glory of his glorified body and accomodating it to their littleness. In the same way he calls this diluting of his sweetness 'his milk', namely, mother's milk, the milk of his breasts, just what is needed for building up his little ones. It is with wine like this that the bride, in turn, rejoices the heart of her spouse, as is clear from his words: 'Your throat is like the best wine.'* Her immediate response is to say joyfully: 'It is worthy of my beloved's drinking.'* Nevertheless, this wine too she gave to the spouse to be blended with the milk of gentle humility and tempered sweetness, which is why she says, 'He set charity in order within me.'* For the same reason, she is told in another place, 'rejoice with moderation, daughter of Zion!',* so that she may know to set bounds and order to her rejoicing.

Finally, as the banquet ends, fruit is served, fresh and dried, and this I take as indicating the delights of praise and joyful thanksgiving. Both fresh and dried are mentioned, commending recent kindness as well as happily recalling the favors of the past. The bride is faithful to her spouse, indeed, 'the heart of her husband trusts in her,'* and she has learned never to let his present kindness obscure her memory of his past. Rather, the further back in time they occurred, the more pleasing to the spouse to find his bride remembering. Her faithful keeping makes them taste all the better to the spouse's throat, because she has not let them go bad, despite the passing of time. Therefore the older the fruit, the more mellow it is, and in some wonderful way, freshness comes from old age, in that it is the older fruit that provides the fresher pleasure.

8. So the bride is right to call the spouse's throat 'most sweet', seeing that it is blessed with the taste of all these different kinds of sweetness. For in butter, as we said above, the benevolence of charity enriches his heart; in honey, the sweetness of his inner glory sweetens it; in bread, love for his Father's will strengthens it; in fish, the gentleness of patience gladdens it; in wine, the newness of joy gives it delight; in milk, a sober simplicity consoles it; in fruit fresh and dried, it is filled to overflowing with the gift of sweet praise in all its forms. There are moreover other sweetnesses without number, beyond the reach of men and known only to that 'most sweet throat', but it is our hope that throughout eternity they will be blissfully revealed to us through him who is the spouse of the church, Jesus Christ our Lord,
who with the Father and the Holy Spirit
lives and reigns, God,
for ever and ever.
Amen.

SERMON THIRTY-EIGHT

The beginning of the thirty-eighth sermon. Of the sweetness of the spouse's throat, and the bitterness of a harlot's throat, namely, fleshly lust. Also, in what way Jesus is wholly desirable, first to the angels, and then to the bride.

Sg 5:16

'HIS THROAT is most sweet, and he is wholly desirable.'*

Not without good reason has it pleased the bride to end the rollcall of her eulogy with this new kind of praise. As we pointed out in the previous sermon, rejecting all the metaphorical comparisons she has up to now made use of, she has torn aside the fictitious veil and decided that this time her praise must be invested in nothing but its own purity. And why, if not because, neither in heaven nor on earth, can she find anything fit to be compared with the throat of her spouse, 'most sweet and wholly desirable'?

2. For that throat is most truly an overflowing fountain of all sweetness, to which nothing can be compared, and he is so wholly desirable, that he is greater than any yearning and more powerful than any desire. In short, in the throat of our Lord Jesus, there is food for all our sustenance, all the support we need for vitality, all the life of our

spirit. Through his throat, all the foods that life requires are drawn down into his interior, which is what we are, his 'interior'. Through his throat the wholesome breath of God, his Spirit, spreads out to make us living and full of vitality. Through his throat we breathe, drawing in his Holy Breath through our continual desire. Finally, through his throat, when his saliva has been swallowed, it passes from our head, which is Christ, right down to us, a life-giving and joyous flavor to strengthen all that is within us.

You, Lord Jesus, understand our needs, you heal our weakness, you give us all that will help us. Through your manifold wisdom, which is the secret sweetness of your throat, you distribute and apportion to each separate one of your members what will bring them fully to life, make them responsive and strong, as far as each of us has need of it.

3. But how wretched the lot of those who have lived so long in banishment from the sweetness of this throat, that they consider it uninteresting and bitter! They claim to find greater charm in the throat of a harlot, namely, the pleasure of fleshly allurement, whose end, says Solomon, 'is as bitter as wormwood.'* When they have smeared themselves with the false kisses of that deceitful throat, they will discover, but too late, how far apart are good and bad, and with what dreadful danger to themselves they have preferred the most bitter throat of a harlot to the most sweet throat of the spouse. Repeated dabbling in deceit makes evil take a

Pr 5:4

hold of the inmost dispositions of the heart, so that it gives rise to 'evil, as from an overflowing source'.* 'Like the dead, now sleeping in the grave,'* they will rise no more, because now they do not want to rise, nor do they hope for it.* And so the grave in which they lie is 'the open grave of their throat.'*

These men have killed in themselves every taste of good, and vice triumphs over wisdom.* As far as goodness is concerned, they are dead; it does not breathe in them even faintly. They busy themselves in one occupation only, a daily perseverance in burying their dead in that wide and open grave. Jesus told the young man, 'Let the dead bury their dead.'* Lift up your eyes, brothers, to this wretched sight, and see how everywhere in the world this work persistently goes forward, as one man corrupts another, 'each man his neighbor'.* Almost as if holding a funeral service, the dead bury one another, and in their unhappiness, each acts towards the others under the cloak of friendship, calling what he does a courtesy. So that they may throw themselves headlong into the pit of sin, each one digs a deep hole for his brother. Each one leads his brother to he tomb, lays him in the pit of sinful attraction, shovels over him the earth of evil habits and, to make his grave more imposing, provides for him a tomb of proud extenuation and unscrupulous excuse.

4. Very rightly, then, and mercifully, did the Lord Jesus speak to the young man who wanted to be his disciple. He called him away from these deadly courtesies, from the hateful

funerals of this kind of dead man, and said without any compromise, 'Leave the dead to to bury their dead.'* It was as if he said, 'Why should you want even to touch the dead? Do not get entangled in the poisonous friendships of this world, where 'a man's enemies are those of his own household,'* and nearly everything a friend does for you turns out to be a snare. 'Their throat is a wide open grave',* an enormous yawning gulf in which to bury themselves, to begin with, and then all their friends. So, 'leave the dead to bury their dead,'* or it may happen that your desire to bury the dead means that you become overpowered by the dead, and it is you that they bury. Rather make friends with the living and with those who are followers of life—and I am life—so that, 'in the way a young man keeps his life pure,'* you may know a wholesome life and have a happy youth. Cross over from death to life. From the grave of worldly pleasure, which opens wide into destruction, stretch out rather to the sweetness of my throat. For it is my throat that is most sweet, not theirs, and it is I who am wholly desirable.'

5. Yes, Lord Jesus, you are uniquely sweet, and at the same time, infinitely desirable. For so many ages already, your holy angels take delight in you, and yet it is as if they were only now seeing you for the first time, so deep is their longing still to gaze upon you. O sweetness 'ever ancient and ever new,'* to enjoy you for eternity is to be constantly aroused to desire, to possess you completely is to be constantly stirred to new

Mt 8:22

Mt 10:36

Ps 5:10

Mt 8:22

Ps 119:9

*Cf. St. Augustine, Confessions 10.27; PL 40:795.

longings. 'O morning splendor of eternal brightness,'* how joyfully you irradiate those who enjoy you! You are always with them, and yet you are always breaking upon their eyes like the 'morning splendor' of the rising sun. Truly, 'one day within your courts is better than a thousand elsewhere,'* because there the noontide brightness of your face is equally the brightness of early dawn. It is noontide because of the all-embracing finality of its immense radiance, but early morning because of its lovely freshness. What an amazing miracle of happiness this is: complete satisfaction that is never endangered, because desire is always stretching ahead of it! And yet there is no room at all for desire to feel unhappy, because of the completeness with which satisfaction abounds. Repletion cannot enter into it, as the longing is always intense, and yet the yearning can know no pain, for its hunger is full of joy.

Surely, Lord, this is what is meant by that blissful and eternal 'circle', of which the psalmist sings, 'You are mighty, O Lord, and your truth is a circle round you,'* a circle of those who 'seek the face of the God of Jacob,'* of seeking and finding, blissfully finding and nonetheless ardently seeking! For round that most true and brilliant light which is yourself, there circles that blessed society of whom you said in the beginning, 'Let there be light, and it became light.'* They cleave to the Truth, and so they become the 'truth'. They most truly circle around you, always seeking your face,* and rejoicing in having found you, they run to you without exertion, they reach you without hindrance, they lay hold of you without pride, they feast on you without repletion, they possess you without possessiveness, they keep you without anxiety.

O Light most desirable, running so joyfully to meet all who long for you! You present yourself so sweetly, and above all that those who desire you could hope for, you grant the complete, overflowing enjoyment of yourself. And yet, by those who enjoy you, you are desired with desire that is always new, and every minute renewed, and they press eagerly forward. You are sought and you are encircled, and it is as though only for the first time, or better, not even yet, they have fully seized upon you. Who can wonder at it? Since your throat is 'most sweet', its indescribable sweetness has devoured them, but at the same time, you are 'wholly desirable', and they enjoy you blissfully. They desire, then, to enjoy unceasingly, so that, as it were in the one kiss of peace, they may experience simultaneously the bliss of desire and the desire of bliss.

6. Perhaps, too, this is the same happy kiss which justice and peace for ever give each other in the glory of heaven.* For justice could truly be described as the passion of holy desire, with which God is loved, and peace could be spoken of as abundance, referring to that peace 'which surpasses all understanding',* even the understanding of those who have been worthy to enjoy it most abundantly. On the other hand, this abundance is not on earth but up above, where there is 'glory to God in highest heaven,'* and 'abundance within the towers of Jeru-

Cf. Ps 85:10

Ph 4:7

Lk 2:14

salem'.* So perhaps we should look for another reason why the bride has called her spouse 'wholly desirable'. It was an understanding of what she herself had experienced, not the angels, that made her choose these words of praise.

When we look at these words, there are two things to be noticed: that she says 'desirable' and also 'wholly desirable'. Now, he is desirable to his bride in the sweetness of his presence and in the pain of his absence.* Especially when he is absent, she longs for him to be present and never stops turning over in her mind how sweet is his desirable presence and what it has meant to her. Obviously, the more painful his absence, the more desirable his presence, yes, and the more lasting his memory, the more self-abasement in the recollection of it, the more passionate the expectation of his coming. Hence the words: 'Your name and your memory in the desire of my soul.'* And it goes on: 'My soul longs for you in the night, and my spirit in the depths of my heart.'* In the truest sense, that soul is a soul of desires, for it is not satisfied with desiring Jesus with all its strength, but it rouses up its 'spirit' and 'the depths of its heart' to the same passion of desire.

'In the night', she says, 'my soul' will desire you. By 'night', she means the absence of her beloved, when his glorious countenance does not irradiate her with its usual serenity, and it is for her spouse to decree whether this night lasts for a shorter or far longer period. But what difference does that make? Surely, she says, I am not to sleep this night away, because 'the bridegroom delays'?* No, the more he protracts his delays, the more shall I protract and draw out my desire! Surely this night is given me to keep vigil, to stay awake all its course, especially since it my duty to watch carefully for the hour of his coming?* He has chosen to keep this hour a secret from me, to help me keep drowsiness at bay. So, she says, my 'soul', the 'soul' that is all loving desire, it is with this that I love you, O Lord my God, and it is this soul that will 'yearn for you in the night'.* It will be watchful in its love, impatient in its longings, carefully keeping vigil until you come.

Cf. Mt 25:5

Cf. Mt 25:13

Cf. Is 26:9

But since my soul on its own will not be able to keep vigil, 'my spirit in the depths of my heart'* will be called upon to aid it in its task. Reason will come to assist emotion, suggesting to it thoughtful meditations, so that 'from the depths of my heart', the memory of your goodness may come lovingly to help me. 'My soul will desire' the desirable face of Jesus, because when he shows it to me, my love increases and my will becomes fertile with fruits of virtue. And 'my spirit from the depths of my heart' will desire him, because he has only to appear, and the spirit of wisdom and understanding which is within me, small though it be, is more fully illuminated with his light and can think right thoughts about him.

Cf. Is 26:9

Furthermore, 'it is good to wait quietly for the salvation of God.'* This soul is confident that in a little while she will have the perfect fulfillment of her wishes, and she sings, 'I will watch for you at break of day.'* She seems

Lam 3:26

Is 26:9

to be saying: I know in whom I have believed,* and I have complete confidence that in the night and in the day prayer is answered. You will not disappoint my hope, Lord. In your compassion you have let me 'watch for you in the night', and by your gift 'I shall watch for you', even 'at break of day.'* Indeed I will keep watch, so as not to lose through my lazy carelessness what I have held. And though I do not yet hold him, I am sure I can win him back by watching and desiring.*

We see, then, that when a soul is lanquishing with love, the Lord Jesus is desirable to it for two reasons. For when his grace is present, it rouses the heart with the desire to hold him, and when he is absent, he stirs up the desire to seek him.

7. But how is he 'wholly desirable'?* To my mind, when she says 'wholly', her intention is to signify that even his very shadow will be 'desirable'. My main reason comes from what she said before, when she spoke to the maidens and mentioned the desires she had of this kind. She said then, 'I have sat down under the shadow of him whom I desired, and his fruit was sweet to my throat.'* Small wonder if, sick with desire, she should believe that the shadow of him she desires, namely, the shadow of the tree of life, should bring her healing. Even the shadow of Peter was once sought after by the sick, and found to give them health.* Also, the shadow of Peter was a symbol of the wonderful power of healing and of refreshing in every way which made him come to help the sick with

no less power than compassion. While that shadow brought health to sick bodies, it was proclaiming with great clarity the strong light that illuminated Peter and so made him cast a shadow. In its very self, it was proclaiming to those whose strength was returning, the strength of the light, as if the shadow itself was telling those who fled to it for refuge, 'Why do you fix your eyes on me, or on Peter? It is not we who do these things, it is the Light, which has shone upon Peter, and so produced me, Peter's shadow.'

If there is such great power in Peter's shadow, what ought not the bride to expect from the shadow of her spouse? But, you will ask, what is that shadow? I think it is the protection, the cool, the concealment, with which he graciously overshadows the soul that loves him, hiding her within the secret of his face.* There it is his custom to shield her, at one time from the glare of fleshly temptation, and at another, from the far more dangerous heat of spiritual sin. It is a gracious shadow, full of saving power, and sometimes, when grace itself seems lost, it comes to our help in the sickness of various temptations, providing refreshment. It is a specially gracious shadow in that it brings back the desirable presence of the spouse for the moment, symbolizing as it does, protection. For a shadow represents what it is a shadow of, by imitating its outline.

Cf. Ps 31:22

So then, there is nothing that is not desirable in him who is 'wholly desirable'. His absence brings healing, his lingering brings salvation, his keeping us waiting brings us

closer to virtue. Under this desirable shadow, the shadow of him she desires, the bride finds rest and comfort. She sits there under his shadow, patiently waiting until some ripe fruit from the tree of life should fall into her lap as she waits. It is impossible that the Lord's bride should be disappointed, because 'the Lord hears the sighs of the poor.'* It has all turned out as she hoped, her destiny has fulfilled all her expectations, and so she says, 'And his fruit is sweet to my throat.'* In this case then, the Lord Jesus is seen as 'wholly desirable', desirable when present, desirable even when absent. His light is desirable, and his shadow, too, in short, everything in him is desirable, everything that has the taste and the fragrance of Jesus, only Son of the Father, spouse of the church, who together with
the Father and the Holy Spirit,
lives and reigns, God,
for ever and ever.
Amen.

Cf. Ps 10:19

Sg 2:3

SERMON THIRTY-NINE

The beginning of the thirty-ninth sermon. An excuse for the length of the preceding sermons. Also, that these words of the bride, which at first appear rather arrogant, on being more closely considered have the taste of humility and love.

'SUCH IS MY BELOVED, and he himself is my friend, daughters of Jerusalem.'*   *Sg 5:16*
Since each of us looks at things differently, we have daily experience of the difficulty of serving everyone as he prefers. Many sit down to table, but there is only one servant, and he has the difficult task of trying to satisfy the taste of every single person. I have said this especially, because some think the word of God should be spoken with brevity, while others prefer everything made perfectly clear.* Many are pleased with the   *Cf. RB 2.31*
intelligent neatness of a sermon, while others are more attracted by the sweetness of the message they find in it. Amid such conflicting tastes, I am sometimes tossed about by conflicting doubts, uncertain whether I am not setting rather uninteresting rations before the sons of the prophets,* that is, before your-   *Cf. 2 Kgs 4:38*
selves. Now, I am quite conscious that in my previous discourses I may have seemed to some to be too wordy, but I can call to

my assistance no ordinary excuse! For, 'the word of the Lord came' by my hand,* that word which rings so fully throughout this bridal song, glorifying the Word.

In the whole of this song, there is no other place where the bride so concentrates all that she is in praise of her beloved, so pours out all her soul, so takes up all the members of her beloved, separately and one after the other, so as to praise them. There is no doubt that the Spirit of charity has breathed more of his sweetness and grace into these same praises than into all the words that follow them. In what comes next, the bride is praised by the spouse or else, trying to draw the maidens to charity, she commends herself to them with motherly affection.

This, then, is the reason why up to now my sermons have been so long, and I am quite confident that any devout reader will have no difficulty in forgiving me. Even if what I have written does not perhaps deserve to be read very often, still, 'my secret is within me',* and 'within my heart I praise the God of my life,'* longing to offer him this sacrifice of praise.* 'To you, O God, I must perform these loving vows,'* and my prayer is that you will stand by me in these vows and reward what I say in your praise, you who enkindle my love and judge my conscience. But I have said enough.

2. 'Such is my beloved, and he himself is my friend, daughters of Jerusalem.'*

The bride has gracefully concluded the phrases of her eulogy, and now turns to the daughters of Jerusalem, glorying that there are two things that give her cause to glory in their presence. One is, that 'such is her beloved', and the other, that although he is such, 'he himself is her friend'. In the first, she share his joy means that she nonetheless rejoices for her own sake. In both cases she calls share his joy means that she nonetheless rejoices for her own sake. In both cases calls him her own, her own 'beloved', or her own 'friend', and if some reason must be given for the difference of name, it would seem that he is called 'beloved', because he is freely and sweetly loved, and 'friend', because he in turn loves her who loves him.

Most richly, then, does she glory, in that she loves him who loves her, and that her beloved responds to her love with an equal return of love. For he proclaims, 'I love those who love me.'* I have called it an 'equal return', in so far as there is a like exchange of love, but of course there is no true 'equality'. There can be no possible comparison between the two measures. Yet whether she loves or is loved, it is all the most gracious gift of him alone, that is, of the beloved. But why exactly does the bride want to glory like this before the daughters of Jerusalem in either of these things, or in both?

3. I listen to St Paul, who 'imparted wisdom among the mature,'* and I find him conducting himself with great fear and anxiety in a matter like this. He spoke of his sublime raptures and divine ecstasies with a certain quiet modesty and in veiled terms, and only at a moment of great necessity. Indeed, he modestly suppressed all mention

Pr 8:17

Cf. 1 Cor 2:6

of his own self. His words are, 'I know a "man", caught up now into the third heaven, and now even into paradise.'* Like a careful keeper of the treasure chest and a trustworthy guardian, he stored away in the testimony of his conscience that glory of his. He did not let even the scent of some other trivial kind of glory come near this glory, saying that he would rather die than let anyone drain away his glory.*

Nevertheless, when that youthful Benjamin came soberly back to his young sons after his ecstasies, whether from paradise or the third heaven or wherever else the Spirit of the Lord had rapt Paul away from earth to heaven, he was urged, and passionately, by the charity of Christ* not to keep completely hidden from them those things that had been revealed for their sakes. This was specially because he perceived it would be useful to them, in other words, in case they came to think less of his apostolic authority. And so at length, as if taking his soul into his hands, with fear and reluctance he surrendered himself to the peril of recounting his own virtue.

Before Paul entered upon this praise of himself, he put this modest preface. 'I wish you could bear with a little of my foolishness, but please do bear with me.'* And again, 'What I am saying I say not with the Lord's authority, but as a fool, in this boastful confidence.'* Then, having spoken at length in his own praise, which brought upon him more embarrassment than glory, as is clear from the words with which he ended, he said, 'I have acted like a fool; you forced into it.'* This is shown even more unmistakably when he confesses that he was given an angel of Satan to buffet him, in case the greatness of the revealtions made him proud.* That great man, aware even in this mortal body of heavenly spirits, did not shrink from confessing before the whole church, both the church then in being and that which would one day come to birth, his having 'a sting of the flesh'.* In another place he speaks more fully of the pricks of this 'sting', explaining quite openly how the law of his flesh fights against the law of his mind.* He gave at last a great cry of misery,* 'Wretched man that I am, who will free me from the body of this death?'* And the sound of this cry is a greater and more splendid comfort to the whole church than the greatness of Paul's revelations! She can bear the yoke of her slavery with greater ease, when she remembers that she bears it together with St Paul.

But what is the point of all this? Obviously to make us marvel at this spirit of freedom in the bride, who feels neither fear nor shyness in explaining to the daughters of Jerusalem the singular privilege of her love. The Spirit of freedom is the cause, and it is also what makes her able to love and be loved. As we have pointed out, when Paul was about to say sublime things about himself, he prepared the way be saying something humbling, and he ended with something even more humbling. He shook his hands, freeing them from any bribe for human glory,* and he acknowledged openly that these self-praises made him not so much glorious as foolish. But for the bride,

2 Cor 12:11

Cf. 2 Cor 12:17

2 Cor 12:7

Cf. Rom 7:23
Cf. Heb 5:7

Rom 7:24

Cf. Is 33:15

it is different. She casts away all veil of modesty, and seems to forget the supernal majesty of her spouse, that his least command makes the pillars of heaven tremble.*
Cf. Job 26:11
She makes no preamble, she offers no excuse, she alleges no need or useful purpose. She simply glories in her friend, while the maidens look on. 'Such,' she says, 'is my beloved, and he himself is my friend, daughters of Jerusalem.'*
Sg 5:16

4. Is he so much yours, O bride, as to be nobody else's, or at least, theirs as well as yours? Surely we would have to think you conceited, whoever you were, had not your beloved himself spoken in your favor. To your praise of him, he replies with equal praise of you, and we find the testimony he bears exceedingly sure'.*
Ps 93:6
His testimony, then, is that you have spoken in a spirit of humility, no less than in a spirit of love. For the glory of your beloved, you cry out sublimely that 'such is your beloved and he himself is your friend', but at the same time, for the sake of your humility, it must have a humble ring to it, only provided it finds a kindly interpretation. For when you say that he is 'your friend', it is quite obvious that you referred to his condescension, rather than your own worthiness. What is the real meaning behind: 'Such is my beloved, and he himself is my friend, daughters of Jerusalem'?*
Sg 5:16
Surely it is to give an unambiguous commendation to the daughters of Jerusalem of the gracious condescension of so great a lord, and to draw their attention to it most carefully?

5. 'Daughters of Jerusalem,' she says, 'your

ears have heard me speak very many things in praise of my beloved. Yet this is more wonderful than all I have said, that, although 'such is my beloved', he has nevertheless stooped to become 'my friend'. The only Son of the Father has surrendered himself in friendship to a sinful woman. The son of the virgin has not been ashamed of the embraces of this Ethiopian maid of his.* He whom the angels desire is not abashed to be called 'friend' by his least and lowliest handservant. That face, in which the heart of the eternal Father takes delight, now has bent down to his waiting woman, longing to kiss her lips with love. And he pays her this honor so frequently, that from now on I can dare confidently to call him, not only 'beloved', but 'friend.' *Cf. Sg 1:5*

6. Henceforth, let no one of you, O daughters of Jerusalem, accuse me of pride, for in glorying before you, I have been moved by love, not by vanity. If 'I have become foolish, you forced me to it!'* For if I am beside myself, it is for my beloved, or if I am in my right mind, 'it is for your sakes.'* Both my self control, and also my loss of it, is all serving for your profit. My beloved has led me into his wine cellar, and there I have drunk as much as I desire.* I have come out from it, and as yet that is a place where I cannot bring you. What I can do, is let you feel the wine upon my breath, making you aware, by its scent, of the sweetness I have swallowed. The sweetness you then taste will draw you too to a fuller and more ardent longing for that sweetness in its fulness.

2 Cor 12:11

2 Cor 5:13

Cf. Sg 2:4

To be full of charity does not imply being

free from compulsion. In fact, is there a want more impelling than that of charity? In fact what is more pressing than the compulsion that springs from charity?* Charity, since that is what I speak of, is what compels me. It is a twofold charity, the charity with which I love my beloved, and the charity with which I love you, O daughters of Jerusalem, and both impel me. Because I love Jesus, I long for him to be loved by everybody. Just as I am ill-fitted to his love, so I am wholly inadequate by myself. His beauty is so lovable, his loveliness so desirable, that it is far beyond any expectation of lovers' wishes, and so it is only fitting that it be desired by everyone in his inmost heart.

My daughters, my passionate love for you, for in a special way you are my responsibility, has laid upon me the need to speak of those things which should rather be wrapped in secret silence, and so I appear before you as a fool. But on your side, you must forgive your mother, and not let what has been done for your sakes, lead you to suffer scandal because of me. I shall gladly endure being thought a fool, on your account, as long as I feel that this is helping you to wisdom. In your progress I find joyful compensation for the damage done to my personal sense of modesty. Furthermore, I recall that in the very beginning I warned you about making judgements of this nature, in case, seeing me arguing with you so boldly, you should look askance at my swarthy skin and think me less beautiful on that account.* I do not fear the judgement of 'men's day',* when I stand interiorly before

Margin notes:
Cf. 2 Cor 5:14
Cf. Sg 1:5
Cf. 1 Cor 4:3

the judgement seat of my beloved. Not without dread do I await the sentence I will see written in his countenance. He knows what spurs me onwards, and if I speak too freely to men of what has been stirred up within me by his Spirit, then it is he himself who forces me to it, yes, and you force me, too!* *Cf. 2 Cor 5:14* So if what I have done has spoiled anything of my beauty, then the charity which took the beauty away, has the power to make it anew.

7. O then, daughters of Jerusalem, do not be careless! Since 'such is my beloved, and he himself is my friend',* you too, if you *Sg 5:16* are not careless, will be able in a little while to make just the same boast! O then, take pains, strive your hardest! Let his gracious condescension towards me, mighty though he is, give you hope. Let the desire to love as I do strengthen you to the same bold confidence. 'As for myself', to tell the truth, 'I do not think I have attained,'* but all the same, *Ph 3:13* I urge you, I beg you, 'I adjure you, O daughters of Jerusalem,'* that you too should *Sg 2:1* hasten along the path I have followed. What at the moment seems to you impossible, God's grace will make very easy, if only you are resolute, not only in fixing your whole desire on him alone, but also in believing that he will strengthen and perfect your desire. For he never fails those who seek him, he never disappoints those who trust in him,* he who is *Cf. Jud 13:17* the spouse of the church, the only Son of the Father; and with the Father and the Holy Spirit, he lives and reigns, God, for ever and ever. Amen.

SERMON FORTY

The beginning of the fortieth sermon. The stages by which the bride persuades the maidens to leave all things and seek the spouse, yet how, without her, they would never dare attempt it, and they humbly beg her to help them.

'WHERE DID YOUR BELOVED GO, O fairest of women? Which way did your beloved turn, that we may go with you to seek him?'* *Sg 5:17*

The bride has spoken very freely, she has overwhelmed her beloved with praise, and the effect this has had on the hearts of the daughters of Jerusalem can easily be seen in this question of theirs. It becomes clear that, while the bride was speaking, the very Spirit of love that possesses her has come down upon them too. In fact, they admit that they have been persuaded to seek the spouse because of what she has said of her previous search for him, how, tirelessly, she pursues her quest at every hour, seeking him when absent or even when present.* When he is absent, she seeks to hold him present, and if he is present, he so often slips away from her between one embrace and another, between kisses.* She has hardly entered upon the delights of his presence, scarcely had a

Cf. Ps 105:4

Cf. Sg 5:6

taste, when he has gone. So the sole occupation of the bride, her daily work, her special overriding concern, is always to seek the face of her beloved. She feels no shame in begging the daughters of Jerusalem to comfort and encourage her in her loving devotion to this task, and she has her reward: she finds what she has sought.* They bind themselves to help her, they do not refuse a solemn pledge of their assistance, and they only ask that she should tell them openly, 'where her beloved has gone, or which way he has turned'.*

Cf. Mt 7:8

Sg 5:17

2. However, there is one point about their words that we must notice and consider very carefully. It is this: they do not say, 'we will seek him for you'. No, what they say is, 'We will seek him with you.'* The promise they are making is to be partners in her work, not assistants, not servants. They are binding themselves to fellowship, not to obedience or even, really, to assistance. And, unless I am much mistaken, this is exactly what the bride intended, this is the very thing that she has long been hoping to hear from the daughters of Jerusalem, that they lay aside all their occupations, and their countless, clamorous cares, to devote themselves henceforth solely to this one concern.

Ibid.

This is the reason why she feels no scruple in revealing to them the wound of her weariness,* for it is her desire that, in compassionating their mother, they too should be wounded with the same sort of blow. She entreats them to support and surround her with the joys of flowers and apples,* and by these means makes it ever more clear to

Cf. Sg 5:8

Cf. Is 11:2

them what anguish her soul suffers from the fire of love. In all this, her motive is plainly to form in them, little by little, through these loving incitements, an understanding of this kind of love, until their eagerness for holiness grows to such a pitch that she may pierce them through with a very deep wound of love. So she spurns, and teaches them to spurn, all empty, worldly consolation as if it were the withered flower of the field, apples that have rotted.* Instead she demands something of the glory of the kingdom of God in their lives, as if from flowers that do not fade, and something of the justice of that same kingdom, as if from apples that do not rot, or at least something that breathes the scent of Jesus that flower on whom rests the Spirit of God, and something of the fruit of the tree of life* on which the angels in heaven feed. Such are the things she looks for in them to provide her with consolation in the pain of her love. When they comply and minister to the refinement of her tastes their love increases in them the taste for these same refinements. From their association with the bride, the maidens become spiritually sensitive themselves, and turn in disgust from the fleeting and worthless pleasures of vanity. Then they can call the sabbath 'a delight',* in other words, far from merely taking a holiday from unnecessary labor, they are even more anxious and pleased to lay aside all useless thoughts and words, and in these consolations, which speak to them of eternity, they find a far more gentle and glorious repose.

When they have become used to these joys,

they are in a fit state to ask for more powerful graces. The bride accosts them more earnestly, or, more truly, she puts a more violent pressure on them, adjuring them with solemn entreaty to tell her beloved how weak and faint they are.* Surely the violence of this appeal expresses the growing vehemence, the almost intolerable heat of love in her heart, which denies the enjoyment of her beloved, not to herself alone, but to the maidens also? How wholly and generously she fulfills the law of love, to love her daughters as she loves herself!* There is no privilege that she wants to keep solely for herself, but all her endeavors are directed to making them imitate her in this intense love, making them her equals.

Cf. Sg 5:8

Cf. Mt 19:19

But the embassy she has laid upon them is so unexpected and difficult that they react to her entreaty with great amazement and uncertainty. They do not refuse what she asks, but, on the other hand, they do not dare attempt what is beyond their power without careful forethought. So, while they are trying to assess the nature of the burden that has been laid upon them, what exactly it is and what it embraces, they decide meanwhile that the bride should have some questions put to her about her beloved. They want to know 'what he is like',* in the hope that there may be something among her words that will reconcile them to this bold undertaking and take away the fear of attempting the unusual. The bride gives eager welcome to the truly humble and befitting modesty of these 'wise virgins'.* She is quick to comply,

Cf. Sg 5:9

Cf. Mt 25:2

weaving together a description in praise of her beloved, a short passage, but full of the craftsmanship of the Holy Spirit.* Her eulogy achieves its desired end, to implant in the daughters of Jerusalem a most profound conviction of the spouse's love. Wholly inflamed now with the desire to seek his face, they can devote themselves to the search for him, longing only to cleave to him.

3. All of this, my brothers, gives us the right to ponder, indeed, gives us the pleasure of realizing, the importance of talking about Jesus, the good it does to cleave to those who love him and 'out of the abundance of their hearts'* speak of him. For if 'faith comes by hearing,'* then surely charity does too? Miracles, in conjunction with the preaching of faith, are powerful in arousing faith, and once love has been enkindled, words of love breathe strongly on the flames. There is a brightness about a word drawn from the vein of charity, and love shows itself in eager, impassioned speech. I can say without fear of contradiction, that there is no sign, whether 'in hell below or in heaven above,'* that has more power to draw me to charity than the living voice of a soul that loves God. And if I am deprived of his voice, then his very face draws me, or, if he cannot himself come, then even the loving and sweet remembrance of what he is [draws me on].

Bar your ears, my brothers, bar your ears against dangerous conversation, and consecrate their use to hearing the word of God.* I repeat, 'sanctify them in the truth,'* for the word of God is truth. When vanity knocks at

the door,* oppose it quickly and boldly, for it brings its own reward,* for, 'the wages of sin is death.'* Every time we listen to evil, it soils and poisons, it makes the ear accustomed to trivialities, makes it wise in respect of vanities and proportionately uninterested in healthy things. In the end, it will make the ear deaf. So then, 'open wide your gates, you princes!'* Open wide your ears, open wide your mouth, 'and let the King of glory enter in.'* Yes, let Jesus 'enter in'. It is not his custom to enter, unless 'the doors are shut',* so that, with the gates barred and bolted against vanity, for with it Truth cannot make his home, the King of glory may consecrate the whole house to himself and claim it as his own.   *Cf. Rev 3:20*
Cf. Is 40:10
Rom 6:23

Ps 24:7

Ps 24:9

Cf. Jn 20:26

4. So then, to take up our theme again, sweetly conversing with the bride is found to have brought the daughters of Jerusalem to a high degree of love. They are quite ready to seek the spouse in concert with the bride, side by side with her. Their only stipulation is that they must first know where they are to look for him. Hence they ask, 'Where did your beloved go, O fairest of women? Which way did your beloved turn, that we may go with you to seek him?'* We shall certainly go to seek him, as long as we seek with you. If we were to try to accomplish so great a task without you, it is all too likely that the one we seek would not show himself. We should probably go astray, and 'wander through trackless wastes,* we should lose heart in our fatigue and weakness, and at last we should be ashamed and sorry that we ever undertook   *Sg 5:17*

Ps 107:40

this work. You have told us what to do, now give us your hand, and we shall follow you wherever you go.* Help us with your prayers, strengthen us with your encouragement, support us with your example, urge us on by your succor.

O fairest of women, we beg you not to abandon your daughters. Let us gaze often into your face, let us hang upon your lips, let us stay close to your holy side. You have labored to produce this grace in us, and the Holy Spirit has worked with you. You have nourished us very tenderly with the milk of your breasts, declaring that you had no knowledge in our regard according to the flesh.* It was not solid food you gave us, but milk, inexpressibly sweet, yet that milk was wonderfully well suited for making babies grow. Its taste was so lovely and invigorating that all other meat seemed to us mere grass, 'and all its glory like the grass in flower.'* And now, through your fostering care, we have matured, we have entered into the strength of a more powerful time of life, so that, by the grace of God, you can now speak to us as if we were spiritual beings.* As for us, when you speak to us of your beloved, we can understand the meaning of this angelic language.

What has happened is that your beloved has heard your prayer, he has taken your spirit from you and placed it within the hearts of your daughters, as once he took the spirit of Moses and gave it to the seventy elders,* or when he gave Elisha a double portion of the spirit of Elijah.* We are on fire

Cf. Mt 8:19

Cf. 2 Cor 5:16

Is 40:6

Cf. 1 Cor 3:1

Cf. Num 11:25
Cf. 2 Kgs 2:10

with rivalry of this daring request of his, and we too, can now long for nothing else, look forward to nothing else, except that your spirit, in which we live, on which we feed, which is our very breath, should ever more increase within us. And until that comes to pass in us, no less than in the case of Elisha, by the life of your beloved and the life of your soul, O fairest of women, we will not leave you.* We shall seek him whom you have convinced us must be sought, and we shall make this our main concern, more than anything else. We shall forget what lies behind us and set all our energies on this alone, in every way we can.* In short, this will be our work, and this will be our repose.   *Cf. Ruth 1:16*

Cf. Phil 3:13

5. Speak out, then, say clearly where he is to be sought. His ways are unsearchable, because, wherever his footsteps go, whether through the sea or the mighty waters or anywhere on earth,* no one can ever recognize them. Yet we believe that, through his Spirit, his path will be revealed to you.* If he comes to us, we do not know from where he is coming, but it will be equally difficult, or rather, impossible, for us to grasp, when he has gone far or perhaps turned away to somewhere nearby. Yet for you, to search out his unsearchable ways is extremely simple, for on you, the traces of his coming and going have been more firmly impressed. In fine, you follow after your Elijah, wisely and watchfully, wherever he goes, so that when you see him departing, you expect a greater outpouring of the spirit.* We know that he departs from you now to go away to heaven,   *Cf. Ps 77:19*

Cf. Rom 11:33

Cf. 2 Kgs 2:9

and immediately he will pour down upon you heavenly blessings. Then, when he returns to you from heaven, it will be to tell you something of the joy of celestial glory.

This is why we always see you as like a man awaiting his master, or better, like a bride awaiting her spouse, 'when he shall return from the wedding feast.'* Your spouse comes out of his wedding chamber* so as to tell you about that marriage feast which is everlastingly celebrated in heaven, and to share it generously with you. There is something else you have taught us. He turns aside, but never for long; he is always in the immediate neighborhood. For you said that two days after when he came knocking, and you rose to open to your beloved, and drew the bolt of your door, 'he had turned and gone away.'* Then indeed your prayers were partly answered. For he put his hand through the lattice, and your body trembled at his touch: your soul melted when your beloved spoke.* So he went away but not far, nor long to be away. He was delivered, to return and give himself to you. He went away from you for an hour, so that, while he tarried, you might use the time to speak to us of him, and 'form Christ within us'.* He went away from you, but only so as to offer us, in you, a greater fullness of himself, to let us enjoy his own self in this present life through you. He went away, likewise, to visit his other little ones, 'leaping over the mountains, bounding over the hills',* as the bride herself has said.

Your spouse took care to 'hide himself

from the wise and learned', but he offers
himself to the little ones for them to know
and delight in,* your spouse who is the only   *Cf. Mt 11:25*
Son of the Father and who, with the Father
   and the Holy Spirit, lives and reigns,
       God, forever and ever.
          Amen.

SERMON FORTY-ONE

The beginning of the forty-first sermon. An expression of grief about the general interdict,* in which what affects the Church of Canterbury and the whole English church, has also affected the Cistercians.

<small>In effect 23 March 1208–2 July 1214. See Introduction to CF 29:8–10.</small>

'WHERE DID YOUR BELOVED GO, O fairest of women? Which way did your beloved turn, that we may go with you to seek him?'*

<small>Sg 5:17</small>

These words of the song come very opportunely, not so much from the view point of poetry, as from that of inducing us to express our grief. Let us leave, for a while, the things of love, let the bride come out of her marriage chamber,* let the sound of music die away, let kisses give place to weeping, for 'he has turned and gone away'. We looked for peace, and no peace came.* Babylon has been treated,* but from that attempt at healing there has come, not health, but a wound struck numb. Indeed, 'slingstones have become wisps of grass,'* for she is no more weakened by frequent blows than the anvil under the daily hammering of the smith.* The reason, or so I believe, that 'the poison of asps is incurable',* is that the asp has learned to deafen itself and shut its ears to the voice of the snake-charmers.* For princes, also, as

<small>Cf. Joel 2:16</small>

<small>Cf. Jer 14:19</small>
<small>Cf. Jer 51:9</small>

<small>Job 41:19</small>

<small>Cf. Job 41:15</small>

<small>Deut 32:33</small>

<small>Cf. Ps 58:5</small>

the prophet says, 'there is no charm',* in other words, these men with poisoned minds prevailed in their wickedness because of their foul actions, and it is this great power to hurt that has won them the title of 'kings'. The church has applied her remedies with all patience and respect, she has poured in oil and wine for the healing of this wound.* But the injury festers, it will endure no medicine. It grows swollen and infected, if treated gently; it is painfully irritated if treated more severely. Only God can judge, and the whole affair is waiting for his verdict.

Cf. Jer 8:17

Cf. Lk 10:34

2. 'And you, Lord, how long will you keep us waiting?'* How long will the punishment that one ruler has deserved fall so heavily upon all? How long will we be commanded to pay back, at such heavy interest, what we have never stolen?* For how long, Lord, will you not even spare the glory of your name, seeming to have repudiated your altar and cursed your sanctuary?* Look at your altar, standing bare and deserted, stripped of its rites and the honor it is due. Your house of prayer,* in which we used to praise you, has become silent, and our voices rise no more in common prayer. You made a whip of little cords, but in the heat of your anger it is those who praise and bless your name that you have driven from the temple!* You seem to have hearkened to the demands of the complaining Jews, for the little ones were praising and blessing you in the temple, and you have stopped the praise and jubilation on their lips.* A halt has been called to the praise of David's Son, 'the melody of

Ps 6:3

Cf. Ps 69:5

Cf. Lam 2:7

Cf. Lk 19:45

Cf. Jn 2:15

Cf. Ps 8:3, Mt 21:16

the harp has become silenced,'* and now David and his musicians play it in the house of the Lord no more. There is an end now to his leaping and dancing before the ark of the Lord, Michol's jealousy is satisfied,* and the Lord's ark, stripped of all its admiration, is silent in its solitary glory, within its tent. After so long an illness, the practice of the christian faith might be thought on the point of expiring, unless help comes to it from the Father of mercies.

Is 24:8

Cf. 2 Sam 6:16

3. What are we to think? The great sacrament of love, and its unique memorial, was given by Christ to his bride at the last supper, when he bade her farewell. He left it to her by way of covenant, to be a perpetual reminder of himself and make him present by deputy, and now, suddenly, it has been taken away from her. He is her 'bundle of myrrh', and they have taken him from between her breasts.* They have taken her cloak from her shoulders, the very men who are the guardians of her ramparts,* to whose protection the spouse entrusted his bride before he went on his journey.* They know themselves what they will be able to say in their own defense when he returns and asks them about their conduct. God forbid that any man should dare to think that any action of theirs has been rash or over-hasty!

Cf. Sg 1:12

Cf. Sg 5:7

Cf. Mt 28:19

May God show us his mercy! Perhaps, when we put forth our hand to the Lord's anointed one * (in fact, to all his anointed ones who range themselves with him in this matter), when we dare to touch them even slightly, it could be that touching them

Cf. 1 Sam 26:11

means we are guilty of touching the apple of the Lord's eye.* Then we shall feel the full force of our rash behavior, or rather, the full force of the Lord's majesty, in his wrath. Far better, that we admit and feel that 'it is the mouth of the Lord'* that has spoken, and that 'the zeal of the Lord' of hosts has done all these things.* The verdict of the watchmen of heaven is just, and we can feel that the sentence pronounced upon us here on earth has first received a heavenly ratification. We feel the wound. If only the pain would at last make us understand what we have heard, namely, that everything God does is very right and just. He has not punished us for our sins as much as they deserve. *Cf. Zech 2:8* *Is 1:20* *Cf. 2 Kgs 19:31*

4. Anyhow, today the arrogance of Israel is its own accuser. 'The enemy has stretched out his hand over all its precious things,'* and the possessions of the church lie exposed to public plunder, with no one to resist or contradict. Today the Lord has made the church an object of fear. With the pious approval of the kings of old, the church used to offer her protection even to the guilty, when they fled to her. But now, today, to our very great grief, there is the scandal of finding nowhere beneath her wings* where we could hide. You would be safer if you fled away from her, rather than try to find protection beneath those wings. Yes, the Lord has taken away her boundary fence, she has been given over to plunder, he has broken down her wall and she has been given over to insult and injury.* *Cf. Hos 5:5* *Cf. Ps 17:8* *Cf. Is 5:5*

Today, throughout this country, it is not

Peter's right, when he sees the Lord suffering before him, it is very far indeed from his right, to be zealous for the Lord, to dare to put him a question and say, 'Lord, shall we strike with the sword?'* The Lord will accept no help from any sword of his. Another sword may threaten, but in answer, Peter's sword is to lie hidden in its sheathe, well concealed. What then happens? The enemy sword, sharpened and polished to the last degree,* goes forth as if it had lost its free will, cutting 'to the right or to the left, wherever its edge is directed'.* It takes no head of office or status or hierarchical position. It not only threatens the clergy in what they possess, but vents its rage at will upon their very persons.

All this shows us that the Lord's anger has not yet been turned aside,* and that they have not yet returned to him who smites them.* We can see the church's face all blubbered and overwhelmed with bitter grief, yet for the most part, she has the tears of mourners on her cheeks* precisely because she does not seek the Holy Spirit, the Comforter, so she has no one to wipe her tears away.* You will find scarcely one in the church who is grieving over what is being done to Christ. Their compassion is rather for their purses, and their complaint is that their luxuries have been laid waste. And yet, how sad, despite their daily scourgings, they never cease to cling, hand and nail, to these things, as much enslaved as ever by their drunkenness and lust.

5. What are we to make of it? The severity

of this penalty is made on occasion by clerics, and frequently laymen, for worldliness. Days and nights are spent in the free and unbridled pursuit of carnal pleasure. These priests have disgraced both themselves and their priesthood by having mistresses, and when the state authority imprisoned the beloved creatures, I feel ashamed to say how the clergy rushed to pay their ransoms. They were not slow in lavishly expending what was only theirs in virtue of their priestly office, for that would seem to them the final disaster, not to have their mistresses. For when these women were made a public show, and they themselves stripped of all they owned on their account, they felt neither grief nor shame. But once ransomed they cling to them all the more intently, remembering how much it cost to buy them back.

In the circumstances, can you wonder that 'the hand of the Lord is still stretched out'?* *Cf. Is 9:12* God sees that up to now, his reiterated chastisements have achieved nothing at all. As Isaiah says, God has given a summons to 'weeping and mourning, to shaving the head and wearing sackcloth.'* Yes, God has given *Is 22:12* the summons, but no one makes any reply, except to say scornfully, 'Let us eat and drink, for tomorrow we die.'* The words that fol- *Is 22:13* low are serious, very serious, more than man can bear to hear.* 'Your sin will remain with *Cf. Ps 130:3* you, until you die.'* And nevertheless, after *Is 22:14* all this, they say that they cannot account for the Lord's slowness in their regard, why he does not fight for them more zealously, why he does not rise up as in days of old and the arm of the Lord clothe itself in strength.* As if they honestly thought that a people of this nature were entitled to have the zeal of the Lord watchful on their behalf! They should rather fear for themselves, that still greater punishment lies in store.

6. But now, let us apply to our own church here the words, 'Where did your beloved go, O fairest of women? Which way did your beloved turn?'* Can he have left the marriage feast for a house of mourning? Perhaps so, and perhaps it is there he expects us to look for him, seeing that we find set before us the bread of suffering, and a cup mixed with tears!* What else can be our fare when he is gone from us, when he is angry with us? So, my brothers, let us lose no time in seeking for him there, because he is always close 'to those whose hearts are troubled.'* Whatever the cup may be that the hand of our Father has prepared for us, we, on our side, to prove we are truly his sons, must not be slow to receive it with filial respect. We cannot listen without great shame and confusion when insulting voices cry out, 'Where is your God?'* or else, 'Come down, sit in the dust, virgin daughter of Zion; sit on the ground, there is no throne for the daughter of the Chaldeans.'* She is no longer reckoned the fairest of women, now that she has been reduced to the status of the rest. Up to now she has been fondled and suckled on the breasts of kings, she has been reared in princely abundance.* She grew in age and she became extremely lovely, which roused the envy of her sisters.* Perhaps this was the

Sermon Forty-One

cause of her downfall, as the prophet says, that she put her trust in her own beauty.* *Cf. Ez 16:15* She advanced to the possession of a kingdom, and this made her vain-glorious, saying in her heart, 'I shall never sit as a widow or know the loss of children.'* And all in a moment, to *Is 47:8* the great delight of all who were envious of her, she was widowed of all her mighty patrons and forcibly deprived of that lofty throne of hers. Now she is driven to put her face in the dust and say,* 'It was good for *Cf. Lam 3:29* me, Lord, that you have humbled me.'* It is *Ps 119:71* good for me, Father, Lord of spirits, that you take away from me my spirit, by which I did not live but swelled with pride.

7. So, Lord, act towards me in your mercy, and take away my life, for 'I am no better than my fathers,'* indeed, I have not *1 Kgs 19:4* even come up to the standard of my fathers. So then, take away my spirit, and, when that is gone, you will be able to send forth your Spirit, and I shall not know within me that you have made me a new creature.* The *Cf. Gal 6:17* breasts on which I used to suck have lost their milk. O Father of the orphans, will you not settle your weaned child at other breasts, greater, sweeter, more rich in milk? You have taught me, and I have learned my lesson, that it is not good for me to make the flesh my support, to rest my weight upon a staff of reeds, that will pierce the hand of those who lean on it.* No, what is good for me, *Cf. Lam 3:26* from this day on and for always, is to lean only on you, the Lord our God, and to wait in silent expectation for your consolation.* *Cf. Lam 3:26* 'You have taken me up and thrown me

aside,'* and then once more you will raise me up on high from my humiliation. Never let it happen, O Glory of Israel, that I ask you for the fading glory of this world or for the consolations of earth. I want you alone to be the glory for which I hope and the hope in which I glory.*

Thank you, O Lord God, for letting us see so clearly that you are with us amidst our lamentations. Thank you for decreeing that we should have the favor, at least once a week, of being fed on our daily bread,* your most blessed body. This was truly fatherly and merciful, as otherwise we might faint away on our journey.* Yes, in your mercy you would not have us faint, and in your own good time, your mercy will send us more generous refreshment. Once again you will give us a daily feast, which now we beg for, in silence and shame, only at rare intervals. But for the time being, God forbid that we should find consolation in anything except the full restitution of your grace, Lord Jesus!

I shall take up my stand at the entrance to the tomb, weeping and waiting for some joyful news, whether from angel or from gardener.* Yet if even an angel from heaven were to say to me, 'Do not weep',* but without showing me Jesus, he would be more likely to rouse my tears than still them. All this time I shall make use of my tears; they will serve as pledge and memorial. 'My tears will become my bread, by day and by night,'* until I find once more set upon my table 'the living bread, which comes down from heaven.'* So, Lord Jesus, do not cease to give me this bread until you come, and oh, of your pity, let that be soon! *Jn 6:41*

8. You have fled from us, O King of glory. You have taken flight, you have slipped away from our world of darkness into the land of your own light, you have withdrawn into your royal retreat, the Father's bosom. 'O Chariot of Israel and its horseman',* I lifted up my eyes to look after you, my Lord, and there came to me a solace for my life's journey, the mantle that covered you, a memento of your presence. Why, when it came to me, have you taken it away? Surely it is not to find out if I truly love you?* Those who do not delight in you when you are present, feel no grief when you are absent and are not roused by a longing to see you soon. But the soul who is your bride, will take the scales of judgement to balance by the weight of her grief the weight of love. Bereft of you, 'whom her soul loves',* she will sit on the earth like the purest of doves, scorning all that is green and growing, only waiting for the day when at last she is privileged to see you and to hear, 'Your cheeks are lovely as doves.'* *2 Kgs 2:12* *Cf. Jn 21:15* *Cf. Sg 1:6* *Sg 1:9*

And now, O daughters of Jerusalem, if your conversation with the bride has brought you any understanding of Christ's love, draw him back with your tears when he departs from you. Entice him home from his journeying with your weeping. When he stays away from you, send him the message of your heavy sighs. When he sleeps, arouse him; when he pretends not to hear, do not leave him in silence. Go on and on knocking until he admits defeat and answers, with all the compassion he showed before, 'I have compassion on the crowd, because now they have been with me for many days, and they have nothing to eat.'* Of course, for a few of us, God in his mercy has some crumbs of the bread of life for our refreshment, but for 'the crowd', there is nothing. For nearly two years now, 'the crowd' has waited fasting, cut off from all share of the sacraments. It is all too obvious that they will 'faint on the way',* and, if their hunger goes on increasing much longer, their hearts will forget all about their homeland.

You know well, Lord of mercy and compassion,* all the fatigues of this 'way' and all its difficulties. You know how great a help against exhaustion, and what a protection from our enemies, is this bread which you have prepared for us. In this bread, your love makes us become one with you, our head, and you bind us closely together with the bonds of faith and charity. This is the sacrament where, in some wonderful way, you prepare the eye of our mind, by the gift of the virtue of faith, to look upon your face, and you offer an incontrovertible pledge of that eternal banquet, the blessed sight of you. Lastly, you have given us, in this sacrament, an extremely great and marvelous favor, that of ranking among your holy ones any of your poor who whisper sadly into your ear that they are in want of holiness.

It is open to the world, that it is by the

frequent reception of this sacramental mystery that your faith triumphs in the world. This is why the coming of 'the man of sin, the son of perdition',* who is envious of your glory, will mean the speedy destruction of your altar. He will be quick to take away, as scripture says of him, 'the continual sacrifice',* for when that is taken away, he will be able to destroy the faith and blot out all memory of you from under heaven. Oh, if only those who in these days carry the ark of the Lord and take the place of the apostles as 'stewards of the mysteries of God',* would hearken to this terrible warning! They have been solemnly told about the provision of a perpetual sacrifice, that it must be perpetual, so that there should always be a fire burning on the altar, as the rites prescribe.* Otherwise, if the sacrifice were to cease, the fire of faith would gradually die down, and in the end it would burn out completely. There must be consideration for the little ones, even in their weakness. They may not be asking for bread, but there should still be a generous supply of it ready for them, I would even say, forced upon them. But now, what do we see? When they ask for it, it is taken away from them, and they have nothing to keep their souls alive. What can they do but lie down and die on their mothers' breasts?*

2 Thess 2:3

Cf. Dan 8:11

1 Cor 4:1

Cf. Ex 29:41

Cf. Lam 2:12

9. So then this is how things are. Yet it is absolutely certain that, even in this state of affairs, the church is in the power of the Spirit of her spouse. We know, too, that she has received a sword from him, 'to exercise justice on the nations and chastisement on

the people, to bind their kings in chains, and their nobles in fetters of iron.'* Yes, even on this earth she sits with her spouse on a throne of judgement, acting without let or hindrance, powerful to make decisions, faithfully 'bringing forth justice'.* And what she declares from that throne is only what she has received from the Spirit of Jesus, in other words, from the one infallible norm of truth. Justice, for her, is to give expression to the decrees of the Spirit of God. But for us, justice is to obey in all humility what she commands, as if it were the voice of God himself,* to the praise and glory of the church's spouse, Jesus Christ our Lord, who with God the Father and the Holy Spirit,
lives and reigns, God,
for ever and ever.
Amen.

Ps 149:8

Cf. Is 42:3

Cf. RB 5:4

SERMON FORTY-TWO

The beginning of the forty-second sermon. What is meant by the 'going' of the beloved, and what by his 'turning away'; and why he is first said to 'go', and then, afterwards, to 'turn away'; and there is also an explanation of what is meant by 'his Father's business', with which he must concern himself.

'WHERE DID YOUR BELOVED GO, O fairest of women? Which way did your beloved turn, that we may go with you to seek him?'*   *Sg 5:17*

The daughters of Jerusalem have two questions to put to the bride, where her beloved has gone, and which way he has turned. The result is that they seem to be proposing an alternative, and the bride is apparently free to tell them either where her spouse has gone, or, on the other hand, which way he has turned. As far as we have any right to make conjectures about his 'ways', which Paul describes as 'unsearchable',* he never goes or   *Rom 11:33* turns away from his bride without advantage to her. He never withdraws unless to provide her with something, to bring back with him from his journey something that will be to her profit. That is why she must wait patiently for him if he is slow in returning. It is surely her interest that is being furthered in the meanwhile, and the longer the journey and the more protracted his absence, the more richly laden with blessings is he restored to her.

2. The gospel is our authority that the spouse did sometimes turn away, has sometimes even gone away. 'Jesus turned away from the crowd,' says the evangelist, 'which was gathered in that place.'* And he says again, 'Jesus hid himself and went out of the temple.'* But you will object that this kind of withdrawal has nothing whatever to do with the bride. These are not signs of love so much as tidings of anger. We find it said, 'Do not withdraw in anger from your servant,'* and to my mind, the speaker is afraid, he mistrusts every withdrawal of Jesus, even the most momentary. But we must take note of those withdrawals of his in which there are no grounds for mistrust. A clear instance is when his disciples were pulling hard at the oars, and 'he came to them, walking upon the sea. He wanted to pass them by,' the gospel tells us.* But they were astonished to see so unexpected a sight, and 'cried out for fear'.* So the unexpectedness resulted in astonishment, the astonishment resulted in fear, the fear resulted in a shout, and the shout resulted in them being listened to with compassion. Being listened to gave them confidence, and confidence in the end gave them the accustomed and long desired presence of Jesus. For the children of grace, then, his turning aside was not in anger but in grace. He kept away for a little while, but only so as to return to them more wonderfully and with

greater grace.

3. Then again, 'when he was twelve years old,'* we find Jesus staying away for three whole days, to the very great distress of his mother and father, (we find Joseph honored with this name by the Holy Spirit.*) We hear of them searching through the streets and squares of Jerusalem to find him 'whom their soul loved'.* Their search for him was not in vain, for he soon gave himself to them most fully, rewarding the loss of a small stretch of time by making his abode with them for many years and most humbly submitting himself to their authority.* Lk 2:42

Cf. Lk 2:48

Cf. Sg 3:2

Cf. Lk 2:51

There is something here which no soul who loves Jesus should merely listen to in passing, and that is the reply he makes, almost in rebuke, when they declare the reason for their anxiety. 'Why did you seek me?', he asks. 'Did you not know that I must be about my Father's business?'* If I am not mistaken, by 'his Father's business', he meant to imply: meditating on God's law, being peacefully attentive to his word, a most active and zealous devotion to understanding his truth, not boldly relying on one's own wisdom but humbly seeking the opinion of others. These things are the first sweet blossoms of a good heart, the promise that in ripe old age, there will be rich fruit. The wise man tells us, 'Speak, young man, only if there is necessity. Wait till you are asked twice, and then make a brief reply.'* Lk 2:49

Sir 32:10

So Jesus in his youth is eager to show the traits proper to his own age, those that reveal him as a boy like any other. He goes to where the doctors are seated, and there, in their midst, he sets up his chair of humility, quite obviously sitting at their feet.* He hides his wisdom by humbly asking them questions, showing them every mark of respect and shunning the least trace of presumption. But by the wisdom of his replies, as though compelled by power other than himself, he involuntarily revealed the hidden treasures of his wisdom. All are filled with wonder,* and he eagerly opened the door to their reverent knocking, running lovingly to meet their zealous search.* And so, very rightly, occupations like these Jesus calls 'his Father's business', because wisdom, which 'dwells with prudence'* and is found in the scholar's reflections, as scripture describes, is occupied, works and plays amidst these things in his Father's presence.*

Though, my brothers, at this point, this should be brought to your attention so that when 'you all come together'* you may be concerned 'to be about your Father's business'. We must set ourselves always to have something on our lips that concerns his Father's will or the glory of his kingdom, something that will help us to serve him better, that arouses charity, that has the savor of Jesus about it. Let us ask questions, reverently, about the things of God, and let us give gentle answers. Let both question and answer be pleasantly seasoned with salt, 'the salt of grace', as the apostle calls it.* Finally, let all your conversation be made perfect with words of great gentleness and peace, so that it never happens that, God forbid, anger and bad feeling find tinder from what should be matter for charity.

4. However, all this is really by way of digression, so let us now take up again the movements of the spouse, his 'goings away', his 'turnings aside'. As we said above, for his lovers both of these are a preparation for greater grace, but 'turning aside' seems to indicate a lapse of time that is brief and secret, one that will see a swift and unexpected return of the grace of his coming. When he was about to suffer, and in three days rise again, he said, 'A little while and you will not see me, and again a little while, and you will see me.'* He was encouraging them to bear patiently the 'little while' of his absence, which was going to be more of a 'turning aside' than a departure or a journey. But there was a journey before him, too, one that he would soon be taking to his Father, when he would bid them farewell, and here also, he gave them wonderful encouragement. What he said was unbelievable, the very hearing of it overwhelmed and crushed them, yet he promised with the strongest expression of sincerity that it would help. 'I am telling you the truth,' he says, 'it is expedient for you that I should go away. If I do not go away, the Paraclete will not come to you, but if I go, I shall send him to you'.* *Jn 16:7*

Jn 16:16

5. Think now, I beg you, anyone who is listening to me, of the joy and consolation that three days' 'turning away' was preparing for the little ones who waited; they were soon to have the unexpected bliss of their Lord's resurrection. And then think of the longer journey, which he afterwards took to the

Father, how that would produce even greater grace and a more generous outpouring of strength. All these 'turnings away', in which he frequently left them alone, from the day of his resurrection until the final day of his ascension, can we not think of them as 'red-hot coals'?* They were coals burning into ashes the worldly affection with which they so stubbornly clung to him, burning them with the new fire of holy love, which would gradually make them forget the taste of the world and experience new delights in the spiritual happiness that comes from Christ.

Every single time the Lord turned aside from them, he came back to them as something new and only then for the first time to be known and appreciated. So unprecedented, so overwhelming was the joy, that faith could hardly compass what was before their very eyes. The witness of every sense assured them with one voice that it was true, but the joy was so great that it forced them to doubt.

The daughters of Jerusalem from their long companionship with the bride, understand then the 'turnings aside' and 'journeys' that the spouse makes. From their own experience, now, they see more deeply into the profound reasons behind his actions, which flesh and blood could never teach them for it has no power to savor them. They engage the bride in conversation, and put their question: 'Where has your beloved gone, O fairest of women? Which way has your beloved turned?'*

6. From his original bride, as I said above, he first turned aside, in one way or another,

and it was only afterwards that he went away. But for the bride who speaks with the daughters of Jerusalem, with whom they speak about the beloved, the very form of their query implies just the reverse: that it is first that the spouse goes away, and then after that, he turns away. Why is this, when they are just starting what they want to discuss, and the blessings that will afterwards come to them are still in their happy infancy? The reason, I imagine, must be that in the early stages of his conversation and in the first flush of her joy occasioned by his visits, the beloved kept away longer and returned later and more infrequently, and the bride discomfited by the disagreeable sensation of waiting, and reflecting the while on the length of his journey, used to complain to the daughters of Jerusalem as though sharers of her joys and sorrows about the length of his absences, saying that her beloved had removed himself too far. However, becoming more beautiful in the eyes of her beloved as a result of a number of visits, sweeter for the kiss she awaited from him, more tender from his embraces and sweeter for the anointing and altogether more desirable, she won the privilege of enjoying his presence more often and in greater abundance. Whereas before he had been accustomed to go away, now whenever he withdrew, he merely turned aside, as though making a diversion without intending to make a longer delay. It is as though he were still saying to the bride, what he said in days gone by to his newly wedded wife, 'Again a little while, and you will see me.'* Also, *Jn 16:16*

'Let not your heart be troubled, nor let it be afraid,'* because I am going and coming straight back to you. I am turning away, not going away, withdrawing for a little while, not departing. I am not going to journey into a distant country, the journey I am taking is in your very neighborhood. For a moment I turn away from you, but only to return to you at once with greater joy; you will rejoice all the more when after a little while, I am given back. In a word, the painful 'turning aside' of the present time will bring forth a 'turning aside' which is as joyous as it is fruitful. Look up, I shall turn aside to you like a river of peace, like a torrent of glory to inundate the daughter of Zion.*

This, it seems to me, is the reason why the daughters of Jerusalem first speak of the beloved as having gone away, and then afterwards as having turned aside.

7. But who is able to explain where the beloved has gone, whether going away or merely turning aside? The question is wholly unanswerable, except only for the Spirit of love. It would be well to refer this question to her upon whom the Spirit rests,* because, apart from her, we shall certainly never find anyone on earth who can undo the clasp that binds this mystery, in fact, who can even unravel the reason behind the question. This is why he who was 'a master in Israel',* heard from the true and only Master, 'The Spirit breathes where he wills, and you hear his voice, but where he comes from or where he goes, you do not know.'* Solomon, too, says that the path of the Spirit is a

mystery,* and David could not trace the footsteps of God,* and Paul describes his ways as 'unsearchable'.* *Cf. Sir 11:5* *Cf. Ps 77:19* *Cf. Rom 11:33*

Yet the bride, who has sat as a scholar at her beloved's feet, shows herself more learned than all such masters in Israel. Having no truck with the noisy babble of speech, breathing only the perfume of her interior anointing by the Spirit, the bride has become able to understand and impart these things. But from me, very needy and poor as far as possessing charity is concerned,* nobody need expect any explanations. I feel no shame in coming everyday to the rich to beg a little food with which to keep myself alive. But we read in scripture, 'Give, and it will be given to you,'* and we know that beggars generously share what they have begged with their companions in beggary. Well then, the little I have been given, I herewith gladly hand over to you!* At least, this will keep you from making mock of my poverty! *Cf. Ps 70:5* *Lk 6:38* *Cf. Wis 7:13*

However, I fear that if I attempt what requires a lengthy explanation in the closing lines of my sermon, I may unduly be constrained. Therefore let this sermon give way to the next and come to an end, thus affording to the next a starting point, to the glory of the spouse of the church, Jesus Christ our Lord, who with God the Father and the Holy Spirit, lives and reigns,
God, for ever and ever.
Amen.

SERMON FORTY-THREE

The beginning of the forty-third sermon. How, from what the spouse says and does when he is present, it can be inferred, by a soul who is learned and experienced in things of this kind, where he comes from and where he is going, and what great profit there is in deductions like these.

RATHER SHYLY and hesitantly, I am coming forward to pay the promise I made you yesterday. I am all too well aware of how limited my ability is in this matter, and I should have thought it better to keep silence and conceal my lack of knowledge,* rather than unveil it by my rash loquacity. Yet, since I did strike a bargain in your presence, for love of you, I shall hold myself to the debt. If there is anything at all that comes into my mind, I should freely share it with you, putting my trust in the Spirit of God and ignoring my own sense of inadequacy.

So then, you are waiting to hear how the bride is enabled to detect where the beloved has come from, and where, when he departs, he is going. To make this clearer, I would ask you to listen patiently to what usually happens here within me, and, I am sure, in much the same way, within most of you. I would

Cf. Sir 20:33

not dare to claim any special experience in these matters, superior to your own. I hope, indeed, I am quite certain, that 'there are some standing here'* who have been marvelously blessed by the Lord with the dew of heaven.

Mt 16:28

2. But I shall begin in a Spirit of fear, for he is 'the beginning of wisdom',* that is, of love. Sometimes it is in this Spirit that my Lord desires to visit me, and then he 'bows the heavens' and comes down.* He sets up 'his throne in judgement',* and commands me to be brought before that dread tribunal where his angels stand on either side. He sets squarely before me my conscience, which I had thrust behind my back,* and he unrolls the story of my deeds, thoughts, desires and motives. He spares me nothing, and it is better so. He touches my soul with effectual power, and with tears of compunction, the insane pride that has defied him melts away into smoke. Terrible in the repeated lightning flash of his justice, like arrows attacking me in battle, he bows down, overthrows and casts to the earth, all the hard false conceit within me. While this lasts, and I stand before so great a judge, what spirit could be left in me, were I not able to bring the cross of Christ forward as my mediator, to claim his blood as my redeemer? I can call as witness the price he paid, when he died to give us life, to prevent him entering into judgement with his servant,* 'in case he reduces me to nothing'.*

Pr 9:10

Ps 18:9
Ps 9:7

Cf. Is 38:17

Cf. Ps 143:2
Jer 10:24

3. It is by the mercy of God that the smoke cloud filling the whole of a man's soul

should break out in tears, and the repeated flashings of lightning should lead on to rain and then, after a little, be followed by the serenity of early morning. I breathe again, in the hope of being forgiven. I feel that for me, justice is being changed into mercy, wrath into grace, and I say to myself in thanksgiving, 'Who knows the power of your anger?'* In the very midst of your wrath, you remember mercy. With joy I call to mind that this is the throne of your father David, from which you judge your poor in righteousness.* You seem to be accusing them, but, in your scrupulous fairness, you are making accusations, not so much against them as for them.* All I read of this throne leads me to see it as 'established in merciful love.'*

4. From this throne, then, I feel my Lord visits me all the more often as he realizes I need visitations of this kind more frequently. If between these visitations, anyone asks me, still numb from the feelings of devotion experienced a few days past, and complaining of my Lord's delay, where he has gone or turned aside, the only ready answer I can find is: 'he has made darkness his hiding place.'* A cloud, not of light but of darkness, has taken him from my eyes,* and now that my love has grown so cold again, I feel I have good reason to fear that perhaps, after all, he has turned away from his servant in anger.* Finally I recall that it was from his seat of judgement that I received his visitation, and I come to the conclusion that he has returned to the judgement seat, so as to visit me again from the same place. There he holds in bondage

the vestige of my reflections, and from her I eagerly wait his regard, until all the old man within me,* vanishes away before the frequent import of fear and the smoking out of my former self.   *Cf. Eph 4:22*

5. But there are times my Lord also comes to me to tell me more joyful things than, for my own part, I had expected or even hoped for. He tells me of the bliss of his incarnation, the love of his passion, the many ways in which he there abased himself to reveal his humility and meekness. When I ponder this well, chewing it ever with an indescribable sensation of sweetness, I think to myself, he has called me to the marriage feast.* And this   *Cf. Mt 22:9*
thought makes everything a delight, everything a glory. All things become fragrant, and each single one of them has a delicate flavor. Yet, in all my happiness at being invited to the marriage feast, I do not forget what my Lord taught us. I take care not to choose for myself too exalted a position, fearing to make a bad blunder in the eyes of my host.* My   *Cf. Lk 14:8*
choice is to be lowly, in fact, to be the very last within the marriage hall,* rather than to   *Cf. Ps 84:11*
go outside, even to the most magnificent of feasts.

6. But, as far as I am concerned, this solemn celebration of the marriage feast comes very rarely, and even then, it is over in a brief minute. I am forced to return to my own poor cottage, while the spouse, as is only fitting, ceremoniously keeps the solemnity all the day, with his friends and companions. But I am desolate, lovingly turning over in my mind the crumbs and fragments that

are left over from the marriage feast, and even those, within a very little, vanish from my mind. At this point, were anyone to ask me, all bereft of grace as I am, where my Lord has gone, I shall reply that he has departed to the place he came from, namely, into his bridal chamber.* It is to there that he directs and invites my zeal and my love, and it is to there, where he so recently honored me by showing himself, that I desire to follow and track him down, as earnestly as I can.

Cf. Ps 19:5

7. And so, there are times when my Lord Jesus comes to me, speaking and 'pleading about the kingdom of God',* announcing everywhere in turn that peace and charity of his heavenly inhabitants, bound together by the strong glue of love. I have no doubt at all, at these times, that he has arrived from that heavenly Jerusalem. He intends, at the very least, to refresh the thirsting spirit, as scripture says, 'As cold water to the thirsting spirit, so is good news from a distant land.'*

Acts 19:8

Pr 25:25

At times when some small refreshment has inflamed my thirst even more, and has opened my mouth still wider to drain the cup, as scripture says, 'he who drinks of me will still thirst';* when, also I feel the state of sweetness disappearing after a little while; for he can stay with me no longer, because I am flesh; at these times, I reflect that Jesus has bidden me farewell, because seeking him and desiring to cleave to him, I faint away, I tire and my strength melts.

Sir 24:29

If however, I do henceforth the only thing left to me, if I chew over the last traces of my thoughts in the desire of my heart,* knocking

Cf. Is 26:8

without ceasing, in the hope that he may not delay to visit me again bringing the gladness of the same consolation, then I find myself following Jesus, so far as I can trace him, to the place whence I remember him returning to me a few days before: using as faithful messengers sighs and prayers with which the spirit of grace will deign to assist my infirmity. For Jesus himself seeks messengers like this, to come and stand before him, pleading for me until I can come myself.

8. Should anyone ask me, while I am waiting the return of my messengers, where Jesus has gone (for I shall not dare, sinner that I am, to call him 'my beloved'), I shall have an answer ready, though timidly and shyly. But I remember his word to me,* giving me unshakable hope, that he has returned to heaven, from where I have utter confidence he will come again to console me. I have every reason to expect that he will come again from the same place that I can recall him consoling me in the past, and I pray and beseech and wait confidently for that consolation.

Cf. Ps 119:49

9. There are times when with a generosity that exceeds my hope, he visits my sinful soul after a long period of waiting. He favors it with an unimaginable revelation of the love of the Father, who 'so loved this world that he gave his only Son.'* So sweet is the mystery that it cannot be explained, but in his overflowing grace, he reveals it, as it were, in a gentle whisper. I stand still, then, weighing up and trying to decide from where my Lord has come this time. Judging from what he is saying

Jn 3:16

in my ear, I see and understand that he has stolen quietly from his Father's bosom, if a sinner may so speak, to tell us truly of his Father and explain what is within his bosom.*

After this blessing, too, the time comes when he decided not to stay with me any longer, and I have not enough strength or virtue to hold him back when he flees or call him again to me when he has slipped away. Conscious of my unworthiness, I acknowledge my defeat, as he hastens away to somewhere that he knows. Reduced to all my former misery, I return to what I was in the beginning, that is, to my dust. But I keep in mind the promise once made to Elisha, and I strive with all that is in me not to let my Lord depart from me without my seeing it.* If that happens, I would lose, which God forbid, the 'double blessing', and I would be deprived of his cloak, which I long for as containing the firstfruits of his spirit.* So, with all the thanksgiving I can muster, I escort him when he leaves me for the place from which he came, and, as far as he will let me, I conduct him on his way, up to heaven to his Father once again. I praise him because he is so glorious, I rejoice because he has visited me, but I breathe a deep sigh because he has been taken away.

10. Sometimes, a sweet intimation of love becomes audible to me, that love with which the Father loves the Son, and the Son in turn, the Father, a love beyond words, even beyond heaven itself. It is more than audible, it is thundered at me, for whenever this chances to

happen, 'the God of majesty has thundered'.* Then I stand transfixed, as if hearing a mighty thunder peal, and I droop my quivering little wings. I am astonished and overcome with fear that from so very far away, in fact, from the highest heavens,* the Father's only Son should have come to visit, on its dunghill, his little worm of a creature. 'How has this honor come to me,'* I cry, that my Lord, whose country is so very distant, has thought of me? May it never happen that I hear from him, as Nicodemus did, that I do not know 'where he comes from or where he is going'.* It was in Israel that Nicodemus was a 'master', and he was still a raw beginner in Christian piety. The old leaven was still working away in his heart, whether because of his magisterial seat, or because of the peculiar claims of the pharisees to righteousness. He had not yet 'purged out the old leaven' so as to make it a new baptism,* and there was reason enough that he should hear something like this from the Master of humility.

No, it was not then a case of 'day uttering speech to the day,'* but rather of wisdom being announced to the night, and in the night.* Nicodemus had not yet anointed Jesus for burial, since Jesus had not first anointed him for grace.* He was still a sensual man, not understanding 'the things that pertain to the Spirit of God',* but infected by the human desire for vainglory. His glance was wavering, and he was quite unable yet to look straight at the face of the true Sun. This is why we read, 'Jesus did not entrust himself'* to him, because he did not trust himself to

Ps 29:3

Cf. Ps 19:6

Lk 1:43

Jn 3:8

Cf. 1 Cor 5:7

Cf. Ps 19:2

Cf. Jn 3:2

Cf. Jn 19:39

1 Cor 2:14

Jn 2:24

Jesus, to have his darkness driven away and be brought in freedom into the light. So he, and men like him, deserve to have said to them, either by the Spirit himself or by his inspiration, 'You do not know where he comes from or where he is going.'* *Jn 3:18*

11. But this does not apply to any soul whose ear the Lord has touched with his holy fingers, and made it hear.* *Cf. Mk 7:33* As scripture says, it can listen to Jesus as to a master.* *Cf. Jn 13:13* The soul who has been anointed by Jesus, now herself anoints Jesus sometimes,* *Cf. Jn 19:39* and follows the true Light, not in the darkness now, but in the full light of day.* *Cf. Jn 12:35* I feel certain that any soul like this has learned for herself how to search wisely, and never to make fruitless inquiries as to where either the Spirit or Jesus come from, or where they go. Certainly, from what Jesus says or does, it is easy to guess, as pointed out above, what place he has come from, and to what place, also, he will retire.

As for me, I am determined to think only good of him; I put my trust in the truth of what he says, that when he comes, his purpose is to make his abode with me.* *Cf. Jn 14:23* Likewise, I believe that when he goes, his purpose is nonetheless to prepare a reception for me in the place where he has gone. For he says, 'I go to prepare a place for you.'* *Jn 14:3* And God forbid that I should be so mad as to remove myself from the happy lot of those to whom Truth made this promise! How I thank him! My lot is in his hands,* *Cf. Ps 31:17* and by his grace, it has fallen out for me most happily.* *Cf. Ps 16:7* Through his goodness, I believe and hope that I am destined for the many mansions which, in his

Father's house, he has built for his many mansion-dwellers.* *Cf. Jn 14:2*

And so, both where Jesus comes from and where he goes, yes, and even when he comes and goes, can be deduced. But for this, the soul must watch very intently, in the way I have mentioned, and she must keep herself free from all other concerns and devote herself completely to this peaceful leisure, which is so demanding. The labor of having watched so carefully any one of these comings and goings will not be wasted, for each separate one of them results in a great reward. In fact, the Lord declares that the servant whom, when he comes, he finds watching, is so blessed that he sets him over all his goods.* *Cf. Lk 12:37, Mt 24:46*
But, as both Elijah and Elisha tell us, that servant, who, when he comes, actually sees him coming, is enriched with a double portion of the Holy Spirit.* The apostles, too, *Cf. 2 Kgs 2:9*
who were privileged to watch and understand both when he went and where he went to, as well as from where he will one day come, seeing him ascend to where he had been in the beginning,* these apostles were enriched *Cf. Acts 1:9*
most lavishly by the sevenfold gift of the Spirit. They were anointed with the oil of gladness above all their fellows.* *Cf. Ps 45:8*

12. In saying all this I have made a complete fool of myself, because it is all infinitely beyond my small capacity. But love, I trust, is both the motive and the theme of what I am writing, and that is strong enough to win forgiveness for my extravagance. Now, of course, it will be well worthwhile to hear what answer the bride makes to the daughters of Jerusalem

when they put her this question, but that must be left for another sermon. May that sermon begin with grace and confidence, through the gift of the Father's only Son, the spouse of the church, Jesus Christ our Lord, who with the same Father and the Holy Spirit lives and reigns, God, for ever and ever. Amen.

SERMON FORTY-FOUR

The beginning of the forty-fourth sermon. That the spouse comes more frequently to visit the heart that has made itself ready for him, and especially if it breathes forth a longing for charity. How the heart we are speaking of is a bed of spices, set out in even rows. What it means for the spouse to pasture in the gardens and gather lilies.

'MY BELOVED has gone down to his garden, to the beds of spices, to pasture in the gardens and to gather lilies'.*   *Sg 6:1*

When the daughters of Jerusalem ask the bride where her beloved has gone, or which way he has turned, when they promise her faithfully to be her companions in the search, she gives them a gentle and humble answer: he has gone down into his garden, to visit the beds of spices. Then she proceeds to give the reason for this 'going down' and 'visiting', that it is 'to pasture in the gardens and to gather lilies'.*   *Ibid.*

I must confess I was doubtful at first as to whom the bride meant to indicate here by 'the garden' of her spouse, whether herself, or someone else like her. Even though she is called 'the fairest of women' by the daughters of Jerusalem,* and also by her spouse, who   *Sg 5:9* calls her 'fairest among women',* (in fact, she can glory in a whole array of titles which the mouth of the Lord has given her:* sister, friend, bride, dove, lovely one*) yet, whoever this beautiful one actually is, may she never be tempted to the presumption of thinking herself better than others. For she would bring no slight stain upon her beauty if she tried to make herself special by an unusual loveliness of face!

2. We have an outstanding and evident proof of this humility, as well as an example of it, in Simon Peter. In the joyful days when they were celebrating the pascal feast, the Lord Jesus put a question to him, whether he loved him more than the others. Peter made a shy and humble reply: 'Lord, you know that I love you.'* He did not deny his love, but he was careful not to claim for himself a primacy of love. There was no failure in bearing witness to the truth, but there was a sensitive rejection of any vanity. Clearly, he had not forgotten how, a little while before, bearing false witness to his own good conscience and vaingloriously boasting of his own virtue,* he had proudly proceeded against the Truth, that is, against Jesus.* Having done this once, he suspected everything that concerned himself. And so, all the evidence, as well as all the judgement on it, he handed over to God, his only true witness and judge. 'Lord,' he said, 'you know everything, you know that I love you.'*

Peter was being questioned by him who sees into the heart and mind.* He was being questioned, I repeat, not just about his feeling of love, but also about how it consorted with humility, and he framed his answer to suit. His humble modesty gave beauty to his confession of love, and he made his claim to love rest, not upon his own word, but on that of Jesus. But he refused to arrogate to himself the privilege of loving Jesus more than anyone else. He would humbly admit to whatever virtue there was in himself, but not be so rash as to assail the virtue of others. Put to the question, then, he emerged with flying colors, and in confessing his love in front of the very Prince of love, he has become, for all lovers of Christ, a perfect pattern of confession, of what they are to say in their hearts when Christ asks them the same question.

3. Be very careful then, you who love Jesus or want to love him, oh, be very careful to avoid the folly of thinking more highly of yourself than of others who share this same favor! Be absolutely certain that you will be put to the question about this subject, in fact, perhaps the question has been put to you already more than once. Take care, lest wickedness deceive itself, and he who questions you 'is not mocked'.* If you want to make progress in charity, or rather, if you are concerned not to be lacking in it, your endeavor must never be to be lifted up about anything in yourself, but always to marvel at what is in other people. Put the kindest construction on others' charity, and keep close watch upon your own.

Cf. Ps 27:14

4. It is easy, then, to believe that the Lord's bride, asked by the daughters of Jerusalem about his movements, answered

them both very kindly and very humbly. She explained that he had gone down to his garden, that is, to console with the gift of his presence any soul who embraces Jesus with a love like her own. She is right to call this soul 'a garden', because there is a border of hedge carefully enclosing it, fragrant with spices and springlike with flowers, all making it very fit for the delights of love.

Generally speaking, however much a garden may be distinguished by grace, Jesus does not visit it often, if the hedge of self control is wanting, if a watchful guard over all the senses has not made a circuit round it, if it is not sparing of speech and mortified in food and drink and sleep. In short, it must take every precaution to safeguard the thoughts and desires of its heart, for from the heart, as scripture says, 'life proceeds.'*

So the bridge looks round in all directions and makes a thoughtful examination for souls like this, on fire with the love of Jesus. She searches for them graciously and often, and this brings her to what she is looking for. She finds treasure, and then displays it to those who share the same grace as herself, saying, 'My beloved has gone down into his garden, to the beds of spices'.* Thanks to the kindliness which she has received from the overflowing goodness of her beloved, she rejoices in this new bride of his. She brings to the attention of the daughters of Jerusalem whatever she may have heard about her, or else, she breaks spontaneously into praise, under the inspiration of the Spirit of loving-kindness.

5. First, then, she praises careful conscientiousness, speaking of it to them as a 'garden', and then recommends duty, moderation and sweetness which she describes as 'a bed of spice'. But at first, this plot is rank with the useless weed of evil inclinations, which grow spontaneously from our earth in wild abundance and which, if left alone, make the beds waste land. So first the bed must be thoroughly cleared with the spade of assiduous self-reproach and the hard labor of reiterated compunction. It must be rooted up, not without much sweat of the brow. Moreover, the soil must be well manured to make it fertile, and the Lord's bride must not think it beneath her to do this kind of servile work,* because her mind should be on making his beds fruitful.† On the contrary, the more she desires to be great, the more must she strive, by day and night, to be meek, through the exercise of humility.

So we find that dung, which would offend the eyes of the beloved if it were inside the house or cloister, has only to be thrown into the seedbed to bring credit upon the bride's industry and zeal. Obviously, when we keep hidden within us all the filth of our dispositions, they grow fetid and disgusting, but let us once bring them to the light through a humble confession, and they are a fine preparation for a rich and fruitful harvest. In a wonderful way, what could lead to unpleasantness, in fact, has actually already done so, the bride makes a source of pleasantness, by putting her sins to good use. What will become foul with neglect if left untouched,

*Cf. Ps 81:6
†Cf. Augustine, Sermon 69.1.2; PL 38:441.

through the constant application of hard work becomes well disposed for a harvest of holy shoots.

6. Moreover, this garden, marked out on all sides by even sides, reveals the virtue of self-restraint, which is the outstanding beauty of any soul that loves God. Not only the interior of a man, but even the face he shows to the world, is adorned by what we might call the reverence that comes from gracious serenity. The grace of self-restraint is the uniform equal partition of the garden, whichever way one looks. It is not puffed up by success, it is not overwhelmed by adversity. It denies no happiness from applause, it does not wither when insulted. It is not all aflame with impatience nor does it give way to wantonness. This is why the bride expressly said 'a bed of spice', and not 'a bed of spices', meaning to signify charity which combines the scent of all the virtues into the one aroma of its breath.

What wonder that the Lord goes gladly to see a garden like this, especially when all round its borders runs the rampart of humility and a mighty hedge of self-control! In these circumstances, nothing uncircumcised or unclean could ever enter.* Even if the serpent did creep in, he would find here a strong woman who has girded her loins with strength.* He would find in her no place to set his fang, besmearing her with venom. As we read in scripture, he will not hurt or kill throughout God's holy mountain.* It will be the other way around, the woman will gain glory from him, when she puts on manly

Cf. Rev 21:27

Cf. Pr 31:17

Cf. Is 11:9

courage and bruises him beneath her heel as he lies in ambush. Her foot will crush his head.* *Cf. Gen 3:15*

Think of this, too, that this garden, rich with blossoming spices, breathing out the love of Jesus alone, is strong enough even to draw him, by the great force of its fragrance, out from the Father's bosom! Indeed, she who here speaks in admiration of another's grace, paid no small tribute to the strength of this perfume when she said, 'When the king was on his couch, my nard gave forth its fragrance.'* *Sg 1:11* Oh, how apathetic we are! Oh, how sinfully sluggish! The Lord Jesus sleeps, whether lying in the boat* or half-conscious on the cross or *Cf. Mt 8:25* at rest on the royal couch of the Father's bosom, but we will not rouse him. So often we are in danger from our temptations, we are suffering from the wild and uncontrollable sea of our spirit, we are actually in that sea, and yet we seem to have quite forgotten that 'the Lord of hosts is with us!'* We do not take the *Ps 46:7* trouble to run to him for help, 'in his hiding place within the storm',* and when everything *Cf. Ps 81:7* goes wrong for us, we do not look for comfort in our suffering. And so we refuse to find our glory 'in the cross of our Lord Jesus Christ'.* *Gal 6:14* Jesus is sleeping in the heavens, and we observe the great silence, and the result is that very rarely does one little drop of that heavenly glory come to us. This is why we are so often tossed about by storms, why the abyss so frequently walls us round, and why, he, who stretches out his hands on the cross, gives us no answer from the cross, and why, at rest on his celestial couch, he does not wake up for us.

But, whoever she is, she is truly the very happiest of women, who, wins such a vote of praise from the Lord's bride, namely the reply that her beloved has gone down into his garden, which is herself, to visit and admire at close hand those beds of love from which far away in heaven, the scent had reached him. He has been aroused, and he has woken; he has been drawn, and he has come down; he has been forced, and he is here.

7. 'He will come', says Isaiah, 'like a rushing stream, which the Spirit of the Lord is driving.'* Of course, he comes as if 'rushing', because he himself suffered no little violence before! He comes impetuously, unexpectedly, overwhelmingly, he comes, in a word, ready to drown beneath his flood. What I am saying is clear enough, I think, but only to those who can judge from experience. He comes impetuously because he comes with force. He comes unexpectedly, because he comes so suddenly. He comes overwhelmingly, because he is 'a rushing river'. He comes ready to drown us, because he is greater than any human mind has the capacity to understand.

8. But then, what is meant by saying that he has entered this garden 'to pasture in his gardens'?* I think that the gardener, who is the spouse, is thinking of sowing other gardens from the seed bed of this garden and from the shoots of this bed of spice, and from their spices and their fruits he hopes for pleasure and nourishment. From these gardens, too, he wants to be able to take lovely and refreshing fruits and spices. So it was in

Is 59:19

Sg 6:1

the beginning of creation, when the Wisdom of God provided all things with their own means of increasing. He lovingly and wisely saw to it that every single thing should have within itself the means of having offspring and of reproducing its own kind.* And in consequence, he looks to find this garden giving rise to similar gardens, which is why he lavishes upon this one all the rich grace of his visits. She becomes enriched, and from this all the others will be fenced in, tended, planted and sown. For 'charity does not seek what is her own',* and likewise she ought not to claim for herself any solitude where she can repose and not use it for the good of her brothers.

Cf. Gen 1:11

1 Cor 13:5

9. Let the sabbath rest be delightful, but let it at the same time be useful. Your own will, as scripture points out, ought not to be found saying one word on the sabbath.* Indeed, the delights of this sabbath are so demanding, require such self-control, that you have to strive as hard as you can, only for the repose of that prayerful peace. Now, if in this your own will is not found, then the greatest religious duty of the sabbath is to have given way to your brothers' will. Let the demands of others afford fulfilment for your own self-renunciation. Duty towards your neighbor will fill the gap left by the denial of your own will.

Cf. Is 58:13

10. Finally, let this garden become, not simply a garden, but, as the spouse says, 'a garden-fountain'.* Let the beds open wide and multiply. Let whatever is springing up in it be transplanted, not just to spring up but

Cf. Sg 4:15

to let 'its scent be wafted abroad'.* If she is truly a bride, let her seek her husband's profit, not her own joys and satisfactions. She shows she is a true bride by giving her spouse children who take after him or after her, letting the features of husband or wife shine forth again in the offspring she has brought to birth.

Sg 4:16

Let not this garden strive to be 'enclosed'* in any sense that means she is open to none but her beloved and offers no entrance to anyone who wants to come in and enjoy the fragrance and flavor of what is within her. It will be no small joy to the bride to observe her beloved moving across to the gardens which she herself has carefully sown with spices, to pasture in them and on them. For in pasturing there he lets us enter deep within himself. Yes, 'the joy of the Lord is our strength,'* and our progress is his great comfort.

Cf. Sg 4:12

Neh 8:10

11. 'To pasture in the gardens', says the bride, 'and to gather lilies'.* For Jesus, to feed is to feed us with the delight of holiness since his joy, as he himself said, is in us, so that our joy may be full.* But he 'gathers lilies', when the inspector of hearts sees these lilies pure and fragrant within us and lovingly watches over them in case they wither or droop because infected by self-esteem. With all the riches of paradise at his disposal, with all the abundance of his grace, our gardener is as it were eager to transplant into his own beloved gardens these lilies, that is, those souls who love him. Like the good

Sg 6:1

Cf. Jn 15:11

gardener he is, when the lilies have produced flowers and are springlike in their brightness and are giving off their scent, then immediately he makes haste to gather them and bear them back to the place of their birth, to blossom there 'throughout eternity, before the Lord'.* For the fiercely burning sun of human praise, and the withering blast of self-complacency, are very dangerous for these tender flowers. They will never be safe until the hand of the gardener cuts them. They are cut down, even though compared with the number and beauty of the other flowers, they seem small and scanty.

Cf. Antiphon at Lauds in the Office commemorating a martyr.

Yes, the gardener gathers lilies, when his bride, like a lovely garden, is bright with great banks of lilies, though also with a dense array of thorns, and he praises her for the lilies. But he is sorry to see thorns in his garden and they prick him to temper the lilies' radiance, saying. 'As a lily among thorns, so is my love among the maidens.'*

Sg 2:2

In this way, then, he does not cut the lilies by their roots but transplants them root and all; for he never ceases to transplant any gift of himself, be it shining holiness, or sweetness of intention and devotion to that garden alone where constant and everlasting joy is to be found, there to be rooted even more firmly. We read in scripture, 'As a garden causes what is grown in it to spring up, so the Lord our God will cause holiness and praise to spring up.'* There those lilies are securely

Is 61:11

planted, there they are firmly rooted, there they are perpetually springing up, there for ever they flower in fadeless glory, to the eternal praise and glory of the only Son of the Father, who, with the same Father and the Holy Spirit, lives and reigns,
God, for ever and ever.
Amen.

SERMON FORTY-FIVE

The beginning of the forty-fifth sermon. How these same words also refer to the bride, and how the spouse 'pastures in the gardens' by enjoying their mutual love. How he 'gathers lilies', by uniting them in the love of Christ, or by continually renewing their chastity.

'MY BELOVED HAS GONE down into his garden, to the beds of spices, to pasture in the gardens and to gather lilies.'*   *Sg 5:1*

I remember saying, in the preceding sermon, that it was not clear to me whether the bride intended to indicate herself by what she said, or else, someone who, like her, is a lover of her beloved. I proceeded as if the meaning she wished us to take was that which referred to another, but now I would be sorry not to apply to the bride personally everything that she here speaks of. In fact, elsewhere in this song, we find her using this same way of speaking in referring to herself. It comes when she is inviting her beloved to visit her. 'Let my beloved come into his garden and eat his choicest fruits.'* And then too, there is the spouse, calling her 'a garden enclosed',* and 'a fountain in the gardens'.†

Cf. Sg 4:16
**Sg 4:12*
†*Sg 4:15*

2. In all this, the bride is giving us a lovely and gracious example of modesty of speech,

talking to the daughters of Jerusalem about herself as if she were somebody else. It is clearly her duty, not only to provide them with a model of fervor in loving, but also of modesty in speaking. And yet, it is more from love than duty, for love drives her more.* This is why Paul, wisest of men, used this rule of diffidence when he came to speak about his ecstasies. He says, 'I know a man who was caught up in rapture, either to paradise or to the third heaven'.* Then, too, 'that disciple whom Jesus loved',* when he wanted to refer to himself, used this very charming expression to identify himself, as if it were his proper name. And he went on to speak of that sacred reclining on the breast of Jesus,* an even more expressive indication of love.

The spouse likewise has been drenched in the same Spirit, and when the maidens enquire where her beloved has gone or turned aside, for they want to watch with her in the quest—in the midst of their questioning—she scents the presence of the spouse as he approaches, and shouts with joy. O Daughters of Jerusalem, my beloved is as the door, do not feel bound by the charge laid upon you! With his usual graciousness he has compassionated my love-longing, and he has saved you from your labor. And so, 'my beloved has gone down into his garden',* that is, into my heart.

3. Yes, 'he has gone down into his garden.' For is there anything in that garden which is not his? It was he who dug round it, he who hedged it in, he who took a hoe to it, he who

sowed and he who planted, he who gave it the dews of his blessing, in short, it was he who made it grow.* From one end of the year to another, his eyes have been fixed upon that garden. One thing has followed another, at the right and proper times, whether it needs sowing or planting, hoeing or pruning. He has seen to it, that everything it needs for its cultivation has its time and method.

Cf. 1 Cor 3:6

In all the work done in this garden, what part is mine? What praise and glory belong to me? I realize that my part is to consent to what, of his own accord, he is doing, a willing consent, but that very will is of his giving, his guiding and keeping. Of myself I am doing nothing, I can do nothing, because, to be perfectly truthful, I am nothing.* So it was he who first dug round me, raising a barricade of voluntary lowliness. He built a hedge around me, enclosing me in with the pure fear of God and a delicate chastity. He worked on me, again and again rooting up the depths of my heart and the inmost parts of my earth. He used all that was shameful in me to enrich my dead clay and make it live. He sowed and planted graciously, inspiring me with holy and fruitful thought. He provided the dews and showers that the seasons demanded, frequently bestowing on me the comfort of his presence. Finally, he brought all these things to their conclusion, he gave the growth, and from the growth, the fruit. For lest this grace come to nothing in me, he never ceased to work in me not only the desire and the ability but also the accomplishment of all these things, ever ripening with his breath

Cf. Jn 15:5

what he originally inspired. So the work of this garden, all of it and every single part of it, is his, and in consequence, so is the glory of all this work.

4. This garden then, for the very reason that he has made himself its gardener, has become for me a garden of delights, though it was once barren and neglected soil. To my thinking, the delights are infinite, because my beloved, holding it to be his garden, rather than mine, is accustomed to go down to it. And lest the serpent should ever slip into my paradise, I know to whom I should entrust the gates, I know to whom I should entrust my strength, for its protection. To keep the serpent out, my beloved himself will drive him away. To foil his deceits, he himself will instruct me. To stop his poison, he himself will breathe life into me. To keep even what he says from corrupting me, he himself will sanctify me with the word of his Truth.

All the same, though I must never be ungrateful for such unmerited favors, and indeed, I never want to be or can be, yet none of you, daughters of Jerusalem, should think there is anything great in me myself. Whatever blossoms in me, from his blessing, is like a small garden of spice, compared with the luxuriant gardens of his paradise in heaven and those fruit-bearing trees. Believe me, my garden of spice is not of many kinds, no, there is just one kind: for I am aware of no merit in myself, unless perhaps, that, to some small extent, I am loving, and know that I am greatly loved in return. Indeed, I can put it more strongly: without any doubt at all, it was he who first loved me, and he gave me this unique, unshakeable proof of his love, that his love should lead to my love.* My poor love returns to my beloved as the sweet scent of his grace. *Cf. 1 Jn 4:10*

5. For what is this garden of mine, where my spice breathes, compared to those great plantations of so many different spices in paradise, that sublime place where Paul was privileged to hear mysterious secrets?* From that day on, that great contemplative broadened out his garden, to make it truly a paradise in which the Lord could deeply delight, a sanctuary in which those unutterable words he had heard would be enshrined. These words, which were not lawful for man to utter, were lawful for him to say to himself, were lawful for him to say to God, were lawful for him to hear, though he might not say them.* Indeed, I think nothing in paradise is more unutterable than the words describing the inner love of God. We may take them on our lips. But only the spouse can utter them. Love is so wholly unutterable that no man can even describe it, or know what it is, because, of all the mysteries concealed within the Son, this is the greatest and deepest in paradise. *Cf. 2 Cor 12:4* *Cf. 2 Cor 12:4*

Once, on earth, Paul heard similar words, when first 'the charity of God was poured out' into his heart through the Holy Spirit who had been given to him.* But when he went up to the very altars of the Lord of hosts,* he drew more fully into himself, to his fullest capacity for grace, the fire of Christ's love from 'the furnace', which is in *Rom 5:5* *Cf. Ps 84:3*

Jerusalem.* As a result, he could come back to us with exultation and cry, 'Who shall separate us from the love of Christ?'*

Whether in paradise or in heaven or on earth, as the bride gazes round on the greatness, the number and the luxuriance of these spreading parklands, she calls 'a bed of spice' that little share of charity within herself, by which she loves or is loved.

6. Now she is rejoicing that her beloved has gone down to her garden, I think because, in his going, he will catch the scent of her sweetness, and afterwards, he will bless this bed of hers. All the same, she feels there is another reason why he goes down. 'He has gone down', she says, 'to pasture in the gardens and to gather lilies.'* This is the equivalent of saying, 'It is not on my account, this visit of my beloved, O daughters of Jerusalem, but on yours. Because he himself has put me in charge of his gardens, and you are those gardens, for the sake of your progress, he has graciously bestowed on me a more abundant and repeated gift of himself, both now and at other times. So, if I should take away from you any one of those gifts which for your sake I gratefully acknowledge have been given to me, I would be guilty. And I would be guilty, not only in your regard, but also in regard of my beloved himself, my beloved and your lover, who bears the responsibility for you.*

And so, my dearest daughters, since you know for what reason the spouse comes whether it be to you or to me: to pasture in you is the real reason for his coming. Be very

Cf. Is 31:9

Rom 8:35

Sg 6:1

Cf. 1 Pet 5:7

careful, in case, when he does come and, according to his custom, looks closely into everything, he finds in you anything lifeless. A sad day for you, and a sad day for me, if he approaches you and you do not welcome him with reverence as the only Son of the Father, as your Lord and God, and do not show yearnings to him who is worthy of such great and deserved honor. What heart will there be left to me, what hope, if he goes away from you fasting and famished? How terrible to expect that curse which Jesus laid upon the fig tree, that time when he was hungry and sought fruit from it, and did not find it!* How terrible, that the very leaves of the fig tree withered away the moment it was cursed; so the failure to cultivate good thoughts leads to an inability to utter anything good. In fact, as Solomon tells us, 'On the lips of fools, a proverb is unbecoming',* and a goodly flow of words is not becoming either.* And Jesus, our Solomon, has this to say to the hypocrites, 'How can you say what is good, when you are evil?'* It is only right and fitting, therefore, that where an abundance of fruit is lacking, the bright sheen of foliage should be shaken off, for those who have a heart that bears no fruit, are dry of speech, yes, and sterile in everything else.

    See, brothers, the abundance and luxuriance of that foliage so much admired by men, austerity of life, austerity of garb, the dignity of silence, the penance of working hard and keeping vigils, the grace of self-control, and any other such badges of holy service. But if these things are not enriched

Cf. Mt 21:19

Pr 26:7

Cf. Pr 17:7

Mt 12:34

by a love of Christ in the heart, are they any more than the showy leaves of the fig tree? Listen to the words of the One who can truly judge men's hearts: 'The man who does not love me, does not keep my words.'* In all that a man does exteriorly, he may show as much greenery as he pleases, yet, if he does not love Jesus, he is not keeping the words of Jesus. Whence it happens, that, after a little, these very practices of virtue, with whose green leaves the fig adorns itself when the sun is growing warm, will become quite dry, like aprons made from fig leaves.* Like the fig tree that Jesus cursed, this tree is more than just dry, it is condemned to everlasting dryness, so that 'never will fruit come from it again.'*

7. So, dearest brothers, if at this point I may take upon myself something of the bride's loving solicitude (though, as far as love is concerned, I can do nothing, or very little), let us be very careful not to find ourselves paying too little attention to fertility and fruit, but too much to leaves and greenery. He who comes 'to pasture in the gardens', looks under the leaves to find fruit. I repeat, it is fruit he looks for, not leaves, by which I mean the fruit of love, which makes us love the living fountain, which is himself, and love ourselves too, within that fountain. Perhaps, up to now, the charity of Jesus has not shone as brightly as it should in the hearts of some of us. But, what about the love of eternal life, the peace of brotherly union, a zeal for justice that is also gentle, a smiling humility and a holy meekness? These are what we can call the fruits of charity. Let me say

Jn 14:24

Cf. Gen 3:7

Mt 31:19

that again: these are fruits, and not just leaves.

But, on the other hand, anger, tale-bearing, envy and detraction, such as there are in some of you—and it grieves me to have to say this*—these things mean the destruction, not only of the fruit, but of the leaves as well. The dryness of heart that follows deliberately turns its ears away from the truth. But it turns itching ears and an insolent wagging of the tongue only in the direction of idle tales, scurrilous jests and detractions. Surely a throat like this is a wide open grave,* to which poisonous slanders taste like the sweetest of foods? It has swallowed up in its depth so many dead men's bodies, and fully as many are the just men or their deeds that it does not hesitate to devour, consuming them by detraction. And so, when they all come together in unity,* it is to a very bloody and cruel banquet. They come together from all sides to share a meal of their brothers' and fathers' flesh and mutually to join in burying this flesh in the grave of their throat.

Turn away, my brothers, from food like this, turn away with a shudder of revulsion and set yourselves to oppose it. Our God is not a God of dissension, but a God of peace and love,* who says, 'I shall destroy him who slanders his neighbor in secret,'* and much more him who does it openly, 'I shall destroy.' The enmity of Christ against detractors and tale-bearers is very severe. Paul says they are 'hateful to God',* and in the psalms, Christ himself announces that he will 'destroy' them.*

Cf. 2 Tim 4:4

Cf. Ps 5:10

Cf. 1 Cor 11:20

Cf. 2 Cor 13:11

Ps 101:6

Cf. Rom 1:30

Cf. Ps 101:6

8. Obviously calling the maidens away from things like this, the bride seems to be urging them to get the fruit of love ready for the spouse who will soon be coming into their gardens. This is why she says, 'To pasture in the gardens and to gather lilies'.* The beloved is certainly 'pasturing in the gardens' when he is given the rich food of mutual love among all those who serve God. And pasturing in them, he 'gathers lilies', when this brotherly love is fragrant with holiness. This is not a community bound together by tale-bearing, as described above, by an unremitting flow of jocosity and the insolence of mirth, by any companionship in frivolity or malice, but it breathes out only a shared sweetness of the Holy Spirit. It is as if the spouse gathers lilies by pasturing, and by gathering lilies pastures, while he assimilates them to himself, their head, each one individually sharing in his Spirit, and by the union of holy charity he makes them all one body.

9. But if it is preferable to regard the lilies as being the radiant whiteness of chastity, the spouse is even more in haste to gather this kind of lily in his gardens, because without any doubt there is someone who will 'scatter' them. 'He who does not gather with me,' he says, 'scatters.'* In all these gardens, it is a rare man who is able to fence his lilies in with so impregnable a protection that it does not occasionally happen to them to be invaded and maltreated by 'the hand of the sinner, by the grasp of the unjust and evil man'.* This is the reason for our daily sighs, why our eyes so frequently fill with tears,

why a painful blush mantles our cheeks, because all too often the serenity of our pure whiteness, which is consecrated to our heavenly spouse, has been dishonored by the grime of carnal thoughts and desires.

Still, for those of us who have taken no care to look after our lilies while they were standing, there must at least be no trouble spared in raising them up when they are down. We must do our best, by the unspeakable power of loving tears, to restore to its first radiance whatever in them has been withered by neglect. This may seem impossible to human power, to make these battered lilies whole again, but it is not impossible for the Word of God, who is our spouse.* Not only can he gather lilies that have been scattered, but he can even make new again lilies that have been completely ruined. 'Help me, O Lord my God',* to take delight in your law from the depths of my human heart. With all your vigor, 'fight against those who attack me',* and who are seeking to disperse those few lilies of yours that are within me. Then 'I will not fear what man may do'* in his eagerness to imprison me in the law of sin, because you are far more able to set me free than he is to imprison me, you are far more able to gather than he to scatter. It is in your power, not only to gather what is scattered but even to gather more than was originally lost. It is in your power to restore the fallen lilies, not just to a snowy whiteness, but to make them even whiter than snow.* It is in your power, not only to give pardon to stains because of the virtue of repentance,

Cf. Lk 1:37

Ps 109:25

Ps 35:1

Ps 56:4

Cf. Ps 51:7

but even to give those virtues the palm of victory. All this is in your power, you who live and reign with God the Father and the Holy Spirit, God,
for ever and ever.
Amen.

SERMON FORTY-SIX

The beginning of the forty-sixth sermon. That these are the words of the bride taking pleasure in her spouse, and they are either cut short by fear that he will soon be going away, or else by a passionate onrush of love, because her joy is inexpressible.

'I AM MY BELOVED'S and my beloved is mine, he pastures among the lilies.'* *Sg 6:2*
These words of the song we find the bride saying in two places, but in the first instance the order of her words is, 'My beloved is mine, and I am his',* and in the *Sg 2:16* second, 'I am my beloved's and his desire is for me'.* The first use of the phrase, in the *Sg 7:10* earlier part of the poem, was handled by the man whose crowning achievement is his commentary on the Song of Songs,* the man *St Bernard of* whose mouth the Lord established 'as a sharp *Clairvaux* sword', whom he appointed to be 'like a polished arrow'.* He was in a true sense, 'the *Is 49:2* bridegroom's attendant',* the friend who led *Cf. Jn 3:29* the bride to her husband, a careful steward in seeing to all that was needed for the joys of the wedding. Among the ranks of cupbearers, at whom the queen of Sheba marvelled,* *Cf. 1 Kgs 10:5* I doubt if there was ever one more prudent and loyal than he, more quick and jovial in pouring out the wine. And in the same way,

he poured himself out, especially in all the words he wrote about this Song, so that he seemed quite truly to have been taken into 'the banqueting house',* and to have received, most suitably, the office of keeper of that house and its flagons.*

Cf. Sg 2:4

Cf. Sg 5:8

If any of us comes forward now, to share in the marriage feast by offering some lowly service to the spouse and his bride, it can only be to act as servant under that great cup-bearer, not to serve beside him. He is there as chief-waiter, and it will be honor enough for anybody else, whoever he is, to have taken the flagons from his hands and, at his bidding, to have handed the wine to the guests. As for me, I shall consider myself very well off if I am found worthy to be counted among his under-waiters, which will give me a chance, while serving, to be actually in the presence of the king and queen, and to use this opportunity of service to be allowed, at least to some degree, to enter into the joy of the wedding feast.

2. But enough of this! Now, with the help of God's Word, let us, if you will be so good, really hunt down what the bride meant by these words! Them she offered to our hearing, but concealed from our understanding, and so left us to investigate the meaning. The literal meaning of the words announces clearly that it carries about it some great mystery of charity, but it is shut up and sealed beneath a clasp. Consequently, it is worthwhile understanding the line of reasoning in these words, which seems to follow from what has gone before it.

I think you have not forgotten the bride's overwhelming sense of bodily distress, the nature and cause of which she revealed to the daughters of Jerusalem. It was to cure this wound that she asked for their help, entrusting them with a solemn message to carry to her spouse.* When they bombarded her with questions as to what her beloved was like,* she fell in immediately with their eager queries, and proceeded, expressly and fully, to relate every single one of his attributes, telling them that 'such is her beloved', and he is 'her friend'.* They went on, asking 'which way he had turned' and offering her the support of their company,* when, amidst the joyful hubbub of this discussion, the spouse quietly made his appearance. He came to lay his healing hand upon that great illness that we spoke of previously, to cut short by the happy circumstance of his own arrival the labor of the long journey which the bride and the maidens had soon to undertake in search of him. And so the bride glowing in the fresh light streaming from her spouse, and as if seeing him now for the first time, breaks forth into words of spontaneous and immense rejoicing, crying out, 'I am my beloved's, and my beloved is mine!'*

Cf. Sg 5:8
Cf. Sg 5:9

Sg 5:16

Sg 6:1

Sg 6:2

3. But I wonder whether even she herself is to be thought of as understanding what she said? Holy ecstasies like this produce a pleasant cloud of unawareness. What has happened is so wonderful, so unprecedented and beyond experience, that it brings with it, for the time being, what could be called an enveloping mist of loving forgetfulness. They

completely lose sight both of themselves and of what they seem to be engaged upon. Hence we find Simon Peter, when he saw for himself the face of Jesus shining with the brightness of the sun and his garments as radiantly white as snow, thunderstruck with amazement at the extreme strangeness of this extraordinary sight.* Peter cried aloud, 'Lord, it is good for us to be here; let us make here three tents!'* But indeed, as the gospel tells us plainly, he did not know what he was saying. He was overwhelmed by a profound alienation of his faculties, because he was seeing something completely unexpected, in fact, up till then, quite unheard of. Compelled to gaze in wonder at the unexpected, he was forced to utter something strange! As these things go too deep for the world to understand them, so what Peter said breaks out beyond what man can understand. If in itself what he saw was not ordinary, then he could find no apt words for it.

4. We find the same thing with the queen of Saba. When she saw 'all the wisdom of Solomon, the house that he had built, the food of his table, the ranks of his officials, and the attendance of his servants, their clothing, his cupbearers, and his burnt offerings which he offered in the house of the Lord, her breath failed her!'* And notice, we have greater than the queen of Saba here, yes, and 'a greater than Solomon here'.* Moreover, surpassing all the spices which she gave to her Solomon,* is the scent of those spices which our Solomon tells us he has handled and weighed and savored for himself. For he

Cf. Mk 9:6

Mt 17:4

Cf. 1 Kgs 10:5

Cf. Mt 12:42

Cf. 1 Kgs 10:10

says, 'The fragrance of your oils surpasses all spices.'* And, indeed a throne was prepared for that queen, a throne of judgement,* to condemn the apathy of a lukewarm race of men! From the ends of the earth she made her arduous way* to seek and marvel at the wisdom which today's race of half-hearted men hears crying out in the streets* and knocking insistently at their doors.* But men today scorn wisdom, and drive it away.

And yet, that first Solomon, with all his wisdom, could not satisfy her hunger to the full. He unraveled all problems and explained all mysteries; he opened out in its entirety all that was in his heart;* he loaded her with gifts, and enriched her with spices, and displayed everything that he had in his treasuries.* But for the mind passionately desirous of true wisdom, however deep it drinks, even until 'living water flows from its heart',* it will still never cease to thirst. In fact, the more it drinks, the greater its thirst!* Is there any wonder then if this queen of ours, the true queen of Sheba, that land of incense and spice, after leaving her own country, that is to say, the innermost depths of her own heart, to seek Solomon, and finally after the discomforts of a long journey, much weary panting and painful sighs of her weary soul, earning the grace to find, to look on, to gaze at, to hold and embrace to her heart's desire, one so much loved, is it any wonder, it should be said of her that her breath failed.* Still less wonder then, for lack of breath her words should fail her too.

5. 'I am my beloved's,' she says, 'and my

Sg 4:10
Cf. Ps 9:7

Cf. Mt 12:42

Cf. Pr 1:20
Cf. Rev 3:20

Cf. 1 Kgs 10:3

Cf. 2 Kgs 20:13

Jn 7:38
Cf. Sir 24:29

Cf. 1 K 10:5

beloved is mine.'* If there were not something lacking in her words, this expression of her devotion would certainly be rather lame, especially in this place, where the bride is enjoying the fulfilment of her desires. Here there is nothing lacking in her bliss except that the beloved does not let himself be held very long, and she groans over her incapacity as yet for the total joy she desires. Very probably, this is the reason why her words are cut short: that the fulness of their sense is supplied by her sighs. A little while before, when the spouse was delaying to come, she refreshed her love-longing, very severe though it was, with flowers and apples.* In the apples she drew in the scent of joy now past, but in the flowers, it was the fragrance of a consolation soon to come that she gave birth to with unshaken confidence. It is much the same now. Having blissfully obtained what she desired, she remembers to be disciplined in her enjoyment of it, and while not forgetting the trials of the past, she gives way to no anxiety about those still to come. So, if her desires are left in suspense like this, how could her words not hang in the balance. She is carried from hope to fear, and back again, as her feelings swing to and fro. She sings in triumph over the fulfillment of her desires, but with humility, and so she does not 'boast about tomorrow',* she does not boast as if adorned in some unique fashion.

Indeed, since she knows that she has been given in marriage to the wisest of men, her 'Solomon', who is the very Wisdom of God the Father, she sings more earnestly than ever of the dangers of losing our self control. This is especially true after he had brought her into his banqueting hall.* She knows at once that she has to undergo the test of whether, amidst her ecstasies of happiness, she has learned to conduct herself with dignity. The spouse gave her this gift, and she glories in it most greatly, earlier in the song, when she says, 'The king brought me into his banqueting hall, and within me, he set love in order.'*

Cf. Sg 2:4

Ibid.

6. This 'setting' of love 'in order', is the balanced judgement that comes from true discretion. It keeps her, as it were, balanced in the middle, between both extremes, that is, ecstatic joy and grief, so that she falls into neither danger. If it goes well with her, she is not thereby made overconfident, and if it goes ill, not overfearful. It is only fitting that the bride of the Word should be the kind of person who is not made drunk by being given the full freedom of the banqueting hall, nor one whom drinking makes garrulous. On the other hand, when she is refused entrance to this same hall, it should not make her upset or annoyed. In her memory, then, she cherishes what has gone before, and she cherishes equally what is yet to come. She subdues the raptures of what she intensely experiences by a certain sedate restraint, so that, when she is carried out of herself, she is not carried away from herself, more than is right. She can therefore, leave herself to pass into her God, without forgetting her weight. She can concentrate with all her heart on what is here and now, without ceasing to think about what soon will be.

The man who was 'after God's heart',* once tasted how great was the abundance of the divine sweetness.* Those who partake of it are granted the favor of being hidden within the mystery of God's presence, far from 'the plotting of men and the strife of tongues'.* He blessed the Lord, who had marvelously revealed his tender love 'in a fortified city',* and then, from that 'unapproachable light',* that same sanctuary, David soon returned to the weakness of his own human mutability. So we see him tempering the excess of that enormous sweetness by thinking about his own trials, and he exclaims, 'I said in the ecstasy of my heart: I have been driven far away from your presence'.* That humble restraint did not go unrewarded, or rather, lowliness led us irresistibly to being raised on high.* And so we find his very next words are: 'This is why you heard my prayer, when I cried out to you.'*

^{Cf. 1 Sam 13:14}
^{Cf. Ps 31:21}
^{Cf. Ps 31:22}
^{Cf. Ps 31:23}
^{Cf. 1 Tim 6:16}
^{Ps 31:24}
^{Cf. Lk 18:14}
^{Ps 31:25}

7. The bride, then, in the very fulfilment of her desires is afraid of speaking, but is not allowed to be silent. On the one hand, she feels a triumphant joy, commanding her to speak, but, on the other, her consciousness of what she is compels her to hold her tongue. In fact, happiness and unhappiness share her between them, and she will stay divided until her beloved breaks down 'the dividing wall'.* He will heal all the love-longing that her sick soul feels for him, when he reveals himself in his fullness. What she wanted to say, what she almost had on her lips to say, was this: 'I cleave to my beloved, and my beloved cleaves to me'. But her bashfulness held her back, it

^{Cf. Eph 2:14}

was too daring, and shy fear curbed the ardent expression of love.

But this is not the fear that charity has driven away from the portals of the marriage chamber.* This fear is not a servant, but a most dear son of God.* He is a coheir with charity, and lives for ever inside the house,* keeping charity itself holy by watching that its footsteps do not stumble. So, when the bride was in ecstasy, it hovered round her lips, and snatched from her mouth any foolish word, before it was actually uttered and became irrevocable. It cut short what her words said; for it halts her joyous banquet in its flight. Very quickly it intermingles with the joys she is experiencing, insistently and urgently repeating: 'Be careful not to go too far!'* Cf. 1 Jn 4:18
Cf. Gal 4:7
Cf. Jn 8:35

Terence, Andria 61

So the bride, embracing her beloved, is in labor, though she cannot as yet bring fully to birth. But the day will come when she does give birth, when now strength comes to help her in her labor pains, through the goodness of her spouse. Then in a happy freedom, she will be able to glory that now, in all truth, 'a man is born into the world.'* The sense we have given to these words would hold good, if we say that she tempered the expression of her joy with the bridle of fear. But if, slackening all such restraints, she is this time to give way to the freedom which is her love's prerogative, so that unbridled she is carried by her own impetus, then the same voice will be heard but raised in jubilation. For we know that the feelings imprinted on the heart by joy are hidden by the shout of happiness, Jn 16:21

and what that shout cannot wholly conceal is prevented from being plainly and fully expressed.

8. The bride now in possession of the embraces she has longed for, says, 'I am to my beloved...and my beloved is to me...'* Then if the maidens persist in asking her, what are you to him, and what is he to you, she has no hesitation in answering, 'Why ask something that no words can tell? What I am when I enter completely into the enjoyment of light invisible, when I say farewell to all this world holds and am absorbed again by the God in whom I began, when I am imprinted with God's likeness in which I was made?* Here on earth I am enabled to experience this, but I am utterly unable to speak about it. Cleaving indeed to my beloved, I am united to him, conformed to him,† I am lodged in his heart, made one spirit with him.* So he is the only one, throughout this present life, who knows what I am to him or he to me. Deep within his heart, a new name is stored up for me, a name his own mouth has given me,* and he has inscribed it on his love, as one stone. But he keeps his secret to himself, not even to me has he chosen to reveal it, until 'he brings time to an end',* that is to say, until the day when we celebrate our wedding ceremony.

9. For my beloved, this time is a time of silence, and for me and you, O daughters of Jerusalem, it is a time of waiting. You are not to be deceived in waiting for something so great, for you are like some delightful garden, pasturing my beloved and yours, among the

lilies.* You both refresh him with your reverent love, and clothe him with your flowerlike chastity. Beautiful indeed, in those beautiful eyes, is the chaste generation that loves him, and he has told us himself, that to be with them is his delight.* Take every care, my daughters and my sisters, to please him as much as you can in these matters. You have made yourselves acceptable to him, and for my part, as your mother, I have betrothed you to him, until that day comes when he, who now pastures on you and from you,* will pasture you, together with me, on and from himself. He is the only Son of the Father,
   the spouse of the church, Jesus Christ
   our Lord, who with the Father and
   the Holy Spirit lives and reigns,
   God, for ever and ever.
   Amen.

Wis 4:1

Sg 5:1